WHERE **IT** LEADS . . .?

Cover Design by Gabriel Jufe
Printed and bound in the United Kingdom by
A. McLay & Company Limited
Special thanks to the staff at Network Languages Ltd.
and my brother-in-law Donald Mann

First Edition Publication 2003
Revised Publication 2004

ABOUT THE AUTHOR

Malcolm R. Piper (the author) has spent the last twenty-five years working extensively in the computer IT industry on an international basis. He has held senior management positions in software and professional services outsourcing companies, and has been responsible for the successful creation and implementation of business development, sales and marketing programmes across many global market segments. He has seen and experienced first-hand the effects of one of the most, if not *the* most, dynamic and rapidly changing industries in modern history.

His principal focus and attention throughout this time involved witnessing the deployment of varying computer software applications within industry, commerce and government. This has given him a broad insight into their use and resulting effect. It is this specific effect which has prompted and inspired much of the contents of this book, raising many far-reaching ethical questions concerning the way we plan to live our lives in the 21st century – sixty years following the invention of the world's first electronic computer.

It is the author's hope that, in reading the following material, reflection upon its implications will be seriously considered.

CONTENTS

INTRODUCTION

The social, legal, political and economic impact of the computer revolution has been felt throughout the world over the past six decades.

In gauging the effect, I have purposely selected only those market segments for analysis which, although they may interrelate to events of a given moment, deal, in my view, with recurring aspects of the human condition.

The sharp contrast between today's instant and spontaneous need for information and yesterday's slower-paced lifestyle serves to demonstrate how the creation of an instantly responsive world demands urgent solutions to immediate problems. In many cases, the solutions which are generated/proposed offer no simple way forward and are often perceived to further complicate an intractable problem, leaving in their wake a number of serious unresolved ethical dilemmas.

The background to these events and issues focuses principally on the dynamic level of change and continuing evolution of the computer IT industry on a global scale. The hardware has become more compact and the software even more pervasive.

The technical and ethical implications are enormous, and I have indicated by example where mankind may eventually lead himself and the technology he creates.

MALCOLM R. PIPER

THE CONTEXT
(Root Module)

Throughout the past half-century, the world has witnessed one of the most profound and dynamic technological achievements ever to beset mankind – namely the advent of computer information technology. For the last 25 years of this period, I have worked extensively within the computer IT industry, requiring me to travel throughout many regions of the world, covering Europe, the Middle East, Africa, the United States, Canada and areas in the Pacific Rim. During this time, many people have asked what I have considered to be the greatest phenomenon created by the evolution of information technology (IT). My response is: the overall combined impact of the individual effects that IT deployment has left as its indelible mark across industry, commerce and government, and our everyday lives.

Because computer information technology has proven to be so widespread, and so far-reaching, particularly during the past decade, it has often been remarked that where the computer IT industry leads, other industries follow. The question is: *where is IT leading us to?*

The Present Context

Many IT industry analysts, notably over the past ten years, have attempted to predict future scenarios affecting society, some of which have proven to be nothing less than red herrings/fallacies. One cited example was the prediction of a paperless society. The fact that we are cutting down more trees (and planting more at the same time) is due, in part, to an ever-increasing number of us who wish to retain hardcopies of our own personal documents (e-mails etc.). This is in spite of us having an alternative means, through distributed, decentralised computing facilities, to transmit and retain (store and forward) information in a complete electronic digital format.

A second example has been the stated belief that we will all generate more leisure time for ourselves due to the concentration of high-performance personalised computing at our fingertips. Needless to say, I don't know of anybody who can honestly claim that they have experienced more leisure time due to the accessibility and use of personal computers. What employers seem to expect of their employees, though, is higher efficiency/productivity output due to the demand/execution of a greater workload in a shorter period of time. Leisure time expectation levels have, therefore, required an adjustment and temperance in sympathy with the reality of today's modern workplace environment.

A third prediction relates to the expectation of an overall increase in productivity across all fields of industry and commerce. Although there have been marked areas of increased productivity and efficiency output, such as in computer-aided design (CAD), computer-aided engineering (CAE) and computer-aided manufacturing (CAM), it remains questionable overall just how proficiently the IT revolution has affected the office automated (OA) environment.

The anticipation was that major new software releases, in terms of both their time-to-market stability and functional quality, would dramatically improve productivity output in the back office/front office environments. The reality is that an ever-increasing number of major new software releases and new updates have left many users perplexed as to just where they are positioned on the overall productivity curve given the need, in many cases, for individual familiarisation with each of these newly introduced software enhancements. The ever-increasing frequency with which new software upgrades and updates have been evoked has, in part, resulted from an attempt to resolve earlier software errors/bugs/glitches embedded within the original software module code designs.

In addition, a further productivity concern has been the emerging new phenomenon of the office computer age identified as the 'digital junkie' who gets a drug-like kick out of sending e-mail.

Such people experience excitement when sending multiple e-mails and suffer withdrawal symptoms if they do not receive a new message at least every five minutes during the working day. They are totally dependent on e-mail and incapable of doing their job without it. The digi-junkie is closely related to the digi-coward, who hides behind computer technology to avoid awkward situations. These unfortunate people are relatively harmless, but the arrival of electronic wizardry in the workplace has given rise to a more dangerous figure – the e-mail bully.

Harassment by e-mail should, it has been advised, be made a disciplinary offence, as the first detailed study of electronic intimidation (commissioned in a study by Novell, a leading computer software communications company) has revealed the frightening extent of the problem. More than 50% of employees have been the victims of 'flame-mails' – abusive or sarcastic messages.

Novell commissioned report:
British company analysis (1997)

Thousands of working hours are wasted responding to or deleting irrelevant messages, according to the survey involving hundreds of British companies. Although people have come to depend on e-mail as a means of instant communication, the human cost is high, with personal relationships breaking down between colleagues who stop talking to each other.

The Novell study/report highlights several cases of victims of e-mail bullying being forced to leave their jobs, including a 50-year-old male civil servant who was subjected to a barrage of electronic abuse by a newly arrived female manager. Their relationship deteriorated so badly that they ended up communicating only by e-mail, despite sitting only a few desks away from each other.

As reported in the broadcasting media during September 2003, the loss in effective employee productivity led the management of one of the UK's most successful mobile phone companies (4U) to instigate a 'no internal e-mail' communication policy as, on average, each employee was calculated to be spending no less than 3 hours a day communicating via e-mail to other internal company employees. In many cases, it was recognised that question/answer e-mails could have been dealt with more effectively by one employee directly approaching another in person and/or endeavouring to reach the corresponding party via phone.

In spite of expressed e-mail productivity concerns and the implications of where this may eventually lead in terms of legally actionable complaints/increased company litigation, coupled with inherent malign software code design issues, the world's corporations are still embarked on/committed to further IT investment programmes. To maintain and enable continued provision for their workforces of just four essential office automated requirements – a good word-processing and Excel spreadsheet capability together with good PowerPoint and Internet interactivity/ accessibility – the world's top 10% global corporations currently spend hundreds of millions of dollars each year attempting to achieve this objective. More money is spent per annum by these world corporations than some of Europe's smaller countries' aggregate each year in terms of their gross national product (GNP) output. Indeed, the judge presiding over the recently contested Microsoft versus US State Government anti-trust hearings in the USA expressed complete astonishment over just how the software support industry had evolved into the mega-multi-million dollar industry it has now reputedly become.

Little wonder with so much financial investment at stake that corporations/companies around the world recognise their total exposure and vulnerability to the global havoc wreaked by what is fast becoming known as the E-mail Time-bomb or Virulent Virus.

According to IDC, an IT research organisation, e-mail has now become the main form of written communication with estimates of more than 15 billion e-mails being sent each day during 2003 with projections expecting this number to rise to 35 billion in 2005. With the vast complex proliferation of the Internet on a global scale, where more than 90% of the world's computers use Microsoft Windows systems, if a virus is constructed to exploit weaknesses in Windows O/S, it can quickly cascade all round the world. The economic impact is enormous with hackers and virus authors costing the world economy, in 2003 alone, $1.7 trillion in lost business, decreased productivity, overtime pay for systems staff, outsourced work that could not be carried out internally and the upgrading of software to protect against or eliminate the virus. What started as a schoolboy prank in 1982 has since turned into an illicit computer industry, with more than 7,000 viruses being written each year. Most are designed to create mischief rather than money, eventually fading into cyberspace, but others are more resistant to remedy.

The 'Sobig F' virus has proven to be one of the more damaging strains, with improved mutated versions spreading rapidly during 2003. Some medium-sized companies reported receiving more than 300,000 e-mails with connecting spams in 24 hours. The 'Love Bug' virus was another example, affecting millions of computers in 2000. In 2004, by far the most virulent and destructive virus to date has been 'Mydoom', which cost businesses worldwide $35 billion in one week alone. The virus crippled SCO's website and was expected to also target Microsoft's. In spite of financial rewards/ inducements offered, no culprit/author has been traced/found.

So serious are the potential economic/safety effects on worldwide financial transactions, medical, airline and telecommunications markets, as well as the acknowledged threats in general to international corporate business, that the FBI, together with other high-profile security agencies, is aggressively pursuing perpetrators of what is fast becoming termed global 'cyberterrorism'.

With this fact in mind, there is a greater realism today associated with support and maintenance costs due to adverse past experience. Future hardware and software upgrades and updates, which make inclusion of greater new functionality/enhancements/

modifications/improvements etc. and attribution to system error notification (SEN)/patches/bug fixes, are planned and anticipated within any new future designed software suite produced by any software vendor/manufacturer (e.g. the recently introduced .Net Developer (DND) from Microsoft). It is therefore expected that by 2010 the combination of all the world's corporations and companies would have spent in excess of US$1 trillion on aggregate trying to maintain just these four essential office automated requirements (a good word-processing and Excel spreadsheet capability together with good PowerPoint and Internet accessibility supported on top of a complex network of communication infrastructure software).

The .NET platform:

Building on the popularity of the Windows operating system and the Office productivity suite, Microsoft is now focused on developing technology for the next-generation Internet. The company's .NET platform will enable businesses to collaborate in order to offer an unprecedented range of integrated and customised solutions, which will enable their customers to act on information whenever they need it.

.NET is both a business strategy from Microsoft and a collection of programming support for XML Web services, the next generation of software that connects our world of information, devices and people in a unified and personalised way. Microsoft's goal is to provide individual and business users with a seamlessly interoperable and Web-enabled interface for applications and computing devices and to make computing activities increasingly Web browser-orientated. The .NET platform includes development tools, servers, building-block services, such as Web-based data storage, and device software. It also includes Passport, Microsoft's fill-in-the-form-only-once identity verification service.

According to Bill Gates, Microsoft expects that .NET will have as significant an effect on the computing world as the introduction of Windows.

The aspects of insecurity and unreliability of computer IT are not always intrinsic within the software module design – sometimes inadvertent insecurity impacting on productivity is evoked purely by human error/accident. Examples of these are only too common and feature regularly in the tabloid press and broadcasting media:

Thursday, 3 October, 2002, 00:27 GMT 01:27 UK
US bank in $4bn clerical error

The US investment bank Bear Stearns entered an order to sell $4bn (£2.6bn) worth of stocks by accident in late trade on Wednesday, the New York Stock Exchange (NYSE) has said. The exchange said the order was the result of a 'clerical error' and should have been for $4m. All but $622m of the order was cancelled before execution, the NYSE said. Bear Stearns told the Reuters news agency that the mistake would have no material impact on the company. On Wall Street, the Dow Jones index closed down 183.18 points at 7,755.61, a fall of 2.3%.

Late trading
NYSE officials said that the erroneous order was made at 1540 (1940 GMT) on Wednesday, 20 minutes before the market closed. Bear Stearns entered an order to sell $4 billion worth of Standard & Poor's securities. NYSE officials said that sophisticated arrangements – called hedges – surrounded the risk from the orders that were carried out. Nonetheless, the order was still 1,000 times more than was intended. A BBC correspondent in New York says mistakes are rare, meaning that, if the firm has escaped an impact at the bottom line, such an error may well be described as clerical but it will also be seen as embarrassing.

Previous errors
Mistakes have been made in market trading before by other companies. In May 2002, London's FTSE 100 index dropped by more than 2%, after a trader typed £300m, instead of £30m, while selling a parcel of shares. In 1998 a Salomon Brothers trader mistakenly sold £850m worth of French government bonds by leaning on his keyboard. And at the end of 2001, shares in Exodus, a bankrupt Internet firm, jumped by 59,000% when a trader accidentally bid $100 for its shares, at a time when its value was 17 cents.

The combination of inherent/intrinsic in-built insecurity and inadvertent user error has led many to acknowledge the reality of computer IT fallibility. It is therefore of little surprise that, when compared to other technological innovations (e.g. television, radio, video camcorders, gramophone, hi-fi, ultrasound plus CT and MRI medical scanner equipment, radar and even the electric light bulb etc.) introduced during the last 150 years, computer IT represents the most *insecure* and *unreliable* invention ever created in terms of the experienced mean time between failures (MTBFs). And yet national governments around the world continue to entrust their nation's greatest secrets to computer IT – military/espionage files, medical records, social security records, tax records etc. (all of which have personal implications for all of us). In addition, banks, financial services and insurance companies continue to maintain financial records on each of their account holders, notwithstanding computer fraud which amounts to a loss each week in the UK alone of more than £2 million – the equivalent of one of the largest private employers/retailers in the UK leaving two of its largest stores open (24x7) 365 days a year and permitting anybody to pilfer any number of goods/products during this time.

Of course, when consumers do legitimately purchase any product from any retail store, an interesting point relating to productivity proficiency is found in the way in which computer firmware (software embedded/etched within microchips) is used to individually scan each product identified with its own unique Universal Product Code (UPC). The UPC constitutes a bar of numeric digits which some technologists, scholars and theologians believe may eventually lead to the control of product distribution on a worldwide level. There are many websites which purport to understand this product control issue. Some even outline doomsday events which have biblical connotations and others which pour derision over such claims.

UPC:
Notably, a number of current websites claim a biblical numeric significance

relating to three sixes (666) – a hidden value integrated within every universal product code. The controversial claim (some believe erroneous) is in the representation of 666 as man's claim to be and emulate God. The triple numeric value of 6 in biblical terms equates to man's attempt to represent the Holy Trinity – God the Father, God the Son and God the Holy Spirit.

An emerging technology ripe for growth in this area is RFD (radio frequency identification), which can replace bar code scanning with short distance data transmission. Because it can collect and transmit a considerable amount of information, the technology holds significant promise to improve manufacturing and supply chain processes (Business to Business – B2B and Business to Consumer – B2C).

The technical capability of centralising and extrapolating numeric data respectively both into and from a common database format, and thereby allowing the creation/deduction of customer profile information such as who purchased what, where and when, is invaluable info to database information companies. In some cases, these are virtual Internet companies who provide information services to market research companies intent on establishing, for example, the success of new and existing products aligned to different social, gender and racial groups drawn from a variety of different environmental backgrounds.

This has led many civil liberty groups to comment upon the effect and significance of holding information in a centralised form, which could lead to an abuse and misuse of power and authority. If the will to implement is exerted, governments of a more authoritarian persuasion could elect to utilise the technology in order to monitor the buying and selling characteristics of each of us. Indeed, some scholars/philosophers and theologians have argued that this is 'Big Brother' and man's attempt to become God. And, if a transition towards a cashless society actually transpires, then, for example, the withholding of credit card transaction capability could leave a targeted individual without the means to buy and sell.

As is widely realised, the pervasive and ubiquitous nature of software design and creation, affecting what appears to be every facet of our everyday lives, has largely emerged from Microsoft's innovation of Windows during the past ten years. To understand how Microsoft has become the highly influential corporation it is, we need to step back and ask ourselves what product creation/marketing strategy/cost pricing paradigms were deployed, which resulted in a company that very few people outside the computer industry had even heard of until approximately 1991/92, and that only became incorporated in 1981, now being the world's largest corporation, with annual revenue for the fiscal year ending 30 June, 2002, in excess of $28 billion, with net income of over $7.8 billion. International non-USA revenue accounted for 27% of Microsoft's total revenues during this period. The corporation is larger than the combined revenues/assets of IBM and Boeing put together. This staggering fact has resulted in William H. Gates, as co-founder of Microsoft with Paul G. Allen, accruing personal wealth in excess of $40 billion as of June 2002, in spite of the prevailing depressed stock market conditions at that time. This, in itself, exceeds the combined individual wealth of all the popular internationally acclaimed rock stars recognised over the past forty years. And his level of personal wealth looks set to increase even further as, according to Bill Gates, Microsoft expects that .NET will have as significant an effect on the computing world as the introduction of Windows.

Even in the hyperbolic world of computing statistics – and just as many other examples could be cited in this book – one other that reaches out and captures the imagination is the fact that the world's second largest computer company to IBM – Digital Equipment Corp., the number one minicomputer manufacturer in the world during the 1950s, 60s, 70s and early 80s – was acquired by a PC company by the name of Compaq in the early 1990s, a company that was only created a few years earlier in the mid-1980s! Since then, Compaq has been working stealthily towards its next large-scale merger/acquisition – this came during the early part of 2002 with its announced merger with Hewlett-Packard. The deal created a giant on the scale of IBM. The new company now dominates PCs and printers, resulting in a broader reach than any other technology company, from stores that sell to consumers to sophisticated back-office equipment. So, in a space of 17 years, from a state of non-existence to a state of global number one existence, Compaq/HP is seen as the symbol of unprecedented demand/growth which potentially has far-reaching effects for the entire global industry and beyond.

The Historical Context

Understanding and unravelling these unprecedented statistics in terms of computer world history is vital if we are to comprehend how and why these momentous events transpired. The origins of early computer design are often referred back to World War II, but even prior to this time the Poles had broken Enigma in 1932, when the encoding machine was undergoing trials with the German army. However, when the Poles broke Enigma, the cipher altered only once every few months. With the advent of war, it changed at least once a day, giving 150 million million million possible settings to chose from. The Poles decided to inform the British in July 1939, once they were unable to break Enigma any longer.

The first break into Enigma came on 20 January, 1940, when the teams working under Dilly Knox, with the mathematicians John Jeffreys and Alain Turing, unravelled the German army administrative key that became known at Bletchley Park as 'The Green'. Encouraged by this success, the code-breakers managed to crack the 'Red' Enigma used by the Luftwaffe liaison officers coordinating air support for army units.

Secrecy shrouded the fact that Enigma had been broken. To hide this information, the reports were given the appearance of coming from an MI6 spy, codenamed Boniface, with a network of imaginary agents inside Germany. While this was pure fiction, there was a real network monitoring the Germans' every move. Unfortunately, the generals did not trust MI6 or its spies and, unaware that the news of what the enemy was doing was coming straight from the enemy's mouth, they ignored it. Nor was this the only problem faced by Bletchley Park. Despite the code-breakers' success in Norway, they had lost the all-important Red cipher. But in May 1940, using a brilliant system devised by a young student called John Herivel, they succeeded in breaking it again. This was one of the most important points of the war. The process of breaking Enigma was aided considerably by a complex electro-mechanical device, designed by Turing. The Bombe, as it was called, ran through every possible permutation in order to try to determine the settings in use.

By the end of 1942 the more complex U-Boat Enigma cipher had again been broken. Yet Bletchley Park's (Station X) greatest success was still to come, with the construction by Tommy Flowers of Colossus, the world's first programmable electronic computer, to help to break the Germans' teleprinter ciphers. Flowers and his team of Post Office engineers built Colossus in December 1943 (the world's first programmable electronic computer, using 2,500 electronic valves), thereby allowing Station X to provide the officials planning for the invasion of Europe with unprecedented detail of the German defences.

The code-breakers also made a vital contribution to D-Day in other ways. The breaking of the ciphers of the German Secret Intelligence Service allowed the British to confuse Hitler over where the Allies were to land. His decision to divert troops away from the Normandy beaches undoubtedly ensured the invasion's success.

But even as the Allied troops waded ashore, a new threat was looming and attention was being given to the role of the code-breakers in the post-war era. After the war finally came to an end, a number of staff continued elsewhere to use the remarkable expertise they had built up at Bletchey Park to break other countries' ciphers, but under a new name, the Government Communications Headquarters (GCHQ). The intelligence-gathering network was aided by the fact that the wartime alliance with the United States continued through the Cold War and beyond. The

12,000 people who worked at Station X did not win the war, but they certainly shortened it, saving countless lives on both sides of the conflict, and their legacy lives with us today with the computer technology that dominates our lives.

One remarkable fact that was released as information into the public domain some forty years following the end of World War II was an insight into probably the world's first attempt to uninvent the inventable – the first electronic computer (Colossus) was dismantled and destroyed under Churchill's command. Although this has been a subject of much speculation as to how and why this came to pass, many believe that Churchill was reluctant to allow secret code-breaking work to continue using Colossus in case the Russians became aware of its existence and thereby conclude that Britain had broken the German military code ciphers.

Given the world's understandable lack of information at that time relating to Colossus, it was assumed, when announced by the United States, that the USA had invented the world's first electronic computer in 1948. Following this American 'invention', the computer's commercial application and potential use was quickly realised, and during the 1950s the formation of International Business Machines (IBM), as part of the Fairchild Group, was created.

Early computer designs accommodated electric valves, which were speedily converted to incorporate solid-state technology with the invention and advent of the transistor in 1956. This quickly led to the evolution of other computer manufacturers, each competing for their respective market position/sector.

One such new company was Digital Equipment Corporation (DEC), which soon established itself as the world's largest minicomputer manufacturer and, overall, the world's second largest computer manufacturer to IBM. Additional, competing mainframe and minicomputer manufacturers also emerged during the 1950s and 1960s, such as Hewlett-Packard, NCR, Burroughs, Sperry Univac and Data General. Together, they became known as the 'Seven Sisters' of the industry, each possessing a mutual respect and understanding of each other's products and services. The result was an effective division of the world market between the seven, each maintaining a loyal proprietary customer base, locking clients into their own proprietary software/hardware designs. This represented a significant financial re-investment programme for the customer should any one single client elect to change from one manufacturer's set of design parameters to that of another.

The advent of 8-bit and 16-bit microprocessor technology during the mid–late 1970s and early 1980s (large-scale integration (LSI) and very large-scale integration (VLSI) – 0.5 to 1.5 million transistors positioned on a single chip) created the backdrop for individual user processing power (comparable to possessing the equivalent of a minicomputer on a desk). This type of capability had never before been seen.

It gave rise to the concept of creating a universal operating system (OS) (overall controlling software 'brain' of a computer, maintaining disk drive and memory accessibility, device driver software modules and application software etc.) which would still provide multi-user, multi-tasking functionality. The desired effect was the support of portable applications. This would allow for the operating system's implementation on a wide range of independent computer manufacturers' hardware designs.

The concept of such a portable computer software 'brain' was developed during the early 1980s by Bell Laboratories in association with a number of American universities. In 1984, the operating system's inception resulted in AT&T (American Telephone and Telecommunications) launching UNIX™ as the world's first truly portable conceived operating system (OS). For the first time in computing history, a common software OS standard using a common portable language compiler ('C' Language) had been created and marketed, with the hugely significant benefit and advantage to the end-user customer, whose investment protection could now be realised/protected. Significantly, it meant that a customer's single reliance on any one single manufacturer's proprietary hardware and operating system design had now been broken. At the same time, it encouraged numerous software developers to develop many different software applications under a common *de facto* standardised operating system. This permitted true migration from one computer manufacturer's hardware designs to another, supporting the same type of operating system. In short, it represented the end-user's optimum dream, but conversely, by the same token, the manufacturer's ultimate nightmare!

Running parallel with the development of UNIX was the earlier mentioned incorporation of Microsoft in 1981. It was at this time that Bill Gates recognised the importance and eventual effect of the next new generation of 32-bit semiconductor integration (ultra-large-scale integration (ULSI) – 1.5 to 2.5 million transistors positioned on a single chip). Its impact would be felt with the equivalent provision of mainframe processing power on a desk, enabling a single user to compute various work applications and so allow transfer of the portable software applications to and from different manufacturers' hardware systems running the same *single-user* operating system. This conceptual idea became reality with the initial birth of MS-DOS from Microsoft and OS/2 from IBM, but was later superseded by the succession of Windows 95 from Microsoft.

It was also facilitated with the portability of communication protocol software to standard emerging communications module cards supporting standard networking 16-bit/32-bit microprocessor chip sets, such as those manufactured by Intel, Motorola, Zilog and National Semiconductors.

These module cards, in turn, have been manufactured to electrically comply with emerging standard 'bus-architecture' designs (hardware back-plane slots that accommodate different computer vendor module cards) such as Multibus I & II, VME-bus and S-bus. The effect has been to consolidate the otherwise many alternative costly computer manufacturers' communication card designs, and thereby, help focus future software development/portability efforts based upon only a few selective *de facto* standards, both in terms of hardware and operating system software design.

Testimony to this fact was and still is seen today in the availability of absolute binary image (ABI) pre-ported software solutions which adhere to the concept of 'load and go', where only one initial portation/development cycle is required to bring a software product to market. The effect is seen in the maximisation of profit as a return on investment (ROI) in the minimisation of time. The speed of technological innovation based upon ROI is exemplified in the creation of very high-speed data communication routers as manufactured by companies such as Cisco and Northern Telecom (NTL). This equipment is recognised as providing the technological backbone to the World Wide Web (www)/Internet, which allows for the transmission and re-routing of numerous differing software applications around the world.

Apart from Bill Gates realising the huge potential worldwide market for such a universally accepted standard single-user operating system, the additional means by which Microsoft became the huge $ revenue generator it represents today was largely due to the new marketing concept of software licensing introduced in 1981. Prior to this date, companies like Apple created their revenue streams principally on the back of selling hardware and software as a combined solution, where the hardware was the revenue-generating factor and the software invariably the zero or marginal cost element. That all changed under Bill Gates' new marketing concept, where the end-user (licensee) paid a licence fee for the right to use and, in some cases, the right to copy software on a limited basis. Under this model, ownership of intellectual property rights (IPR) still remained solely with the licensor (Microsoft) (non-transferable). The rest, as they say, is history, where the software industry continued to evolve and flourish by adopting/emulating the same marketing paradigm as initially introduced by Bill Gates.

IPR:
Interestingly enough, the computer industry had taken its lead from the publishing and music/entertainment industries as far as the claim of intellectual property rights (IPR) was concerned. In both these industries, the author and singer/song-writer retained IPR but, at the same time, relinquished control over copyright protection

and transferred this right to a third party, namely the publisher and record company respectively. The startling difference in the computer industry was that, essentially since 1981, both IPR and copyright protection were retained by the original software author/developer/company (licensor). Indeed, even modifications/ enhancements to the original software product code developed/instigated by a procuring third party (licensee/sub-licensee) still remained the strict IPR of the original licensor, the restriction being that, without the original software developed product code, it would not be possible for the licensee to develop the required modifications/enhancements, hence the legal argument for the licensor to automatically assume ownership of such mods/enhancements unless exploitation rights are otherwise granted/surrendered/agreed to by the licensor in advance/ subsequent to such mods/enhancements developed by the licensee/sub-licensee. In some countries, however (e.g. the USA), the software author does have to surrender both IPR and copyright in situations where such orginal code design and/or mods/enhancements were commissioned by a third party, e.g. a bank, and where the particular bank in question is naturally concerned that an exact replication or near copy of the initial commissioned developed code work could also be sold to a competing financial institution. This practice was made illegal in the USA during 1991/92. However, many other countries have yet to follow this commercial/legal lead, as instigated in the USA.

The Future Context

Some people today have expressed the belief that it is time to move to alternative market growth areas such as biotechnology, that computer technology has had its day and that everybody in the modern world who wants a computer already possesses one, with enough processing power for their needs. There are even claims that engineers have exhausted new ideas of things to invent, although there are many who clearly still do not subscribe to this view.

A number of people (and even some in the IT industry) have either forgotten or have simply discarded the fact that the past 25 years of computing laid just the foundation for the real change, which is to convert all today's analogue systems to digital. They focus on one aspect of the personal computer rather than seeing the Internet as a massive network where all digital applications can be accessed by a wide range of devices. In many cases these devices are expected to comply with electrical telemetry interface standards ('blue-tooth' specifications).

We still have a long way to go to transpose from analogue to digital and, in so doing, still require major innovations just to create high-speed pipelines, both fixed and wireless. One promising technology is the imminent launching of private enterprises in the United States which are anticipated to provide high-speed Internet connectivity over the power grid systems. One such enterprise commenced as early as the autumn of 2003.

The market is still several years from producing fast wireless connections secure enough for businesses to use confidently. There are, however, various exciting wireless projects in the pipeline from start-ups in the United States.

Although today (2004) enterprise computing has barely started the move from traditional client–server-based architecture to web services that will put the Internet at the centre of next-generation applications, it is recognised that increased financial investment has begun to pave the way. As referenced earlier, IT spending is expected to double over the next three to seven years (expectations are it will hit $1 trillion by 2010) in order to cover the purchase cost of many of these new directional developments.

With an ever-increasing demand set to only magnify digital data transmission problems, it is anticipated that today's Internet infrastructure would grind to a halt if left unchecked. Even advance Internet project designs for the next-generation infrastructure may not be sufficient to handle the future digital needs of the globe. Some industry leaders believe it could be obsolete within seven years of going live. The digital domestic home, with its convergence of radio, TV, hi-fi, computing, the Internet and unplugged 'Wi-Fi' technology, is predicted to escalate consumer spending over the next three to five years. By the end of this decade (2010) it is anticipated that almost 80% of our individual work and leisure time will be spent viewing either a glass d.p.i., plasma, LED or LCD screen due principally to the advent of new Personal Application Devices (PADs), voice/video landline and mobile phones, recordable RW-DVD movies, CD games and flat widescreen TV technology coupled with future new generations of portable laptop/palmtop/ fixed-location computers and new developed lines of domestic electrical appliances. In addition, artificial intelligence (voice recognition) 'command' systems for home use are a further projection bound to influence spending as consumers look to invest progressively over the next decade in labour-saving devices that decrease domestic workloads.

Within industry and commerce, there are reasons to believe IT spending will jump as early as the first quarter of 2004. IT directors who overspent on hardware and software in 1998 and 1999 to see them through the Y2K 'doomsday' scenario are now finding that they are seriously obsolete. Servers bought during this time cannot handle industrial-strength web services, and desktop PCs, although still good for basic Internet connectivity, are significantly underpowered to handle the next generation of new applications and services.

Interestingly, recent fraudulent accounting practice scandals such as Enron and WorldCom etc. could soon lead the way for a change in business practices. A number of IT managers are now beginning to secure money for vital sales and field-force automation applications. Chief finance officers (CFOs) are finally acknowledging the need to purchase, explaining that many IT managers are becoming fearful of not having up-to-date information in their systems enabling them to produce accurate forecasts and financial statements.

A number of qualified IT industry analysts who spend much of their time analysing various technology directions/projections continue to highlight emerging technologies.

Microsoft:
Microsoft Chairman and Chief Software Architect Bill Gates used his keynote address at the first Microsoft Mobile Developer Conference to signal Microsoft's intention to play a major role in the digital mobile software business. The software maker intends to make it easy for developers to create applications for platforms ranging from PCs, laptops, palmtops and electronic PADs to intelligent wireless wristwatches and 3G colour mobile phones using the .Net Developer environment and 'blue-tooth' standardisation.

The overwhelming evidence supporting the pervasive nature of readily available software programs supported under Windows is testimony to its global widespread use. These specific software deployments, using industry-standard IT microchip hardware, now lead the world today into uncharted waters affecting many areas of our lives. This, in turn, leads us to seriously contemplate the following . . .

HEALTHCARE MANAGEMENT
(Module 1)

Since its inception in 1948, Britain's National Health Service (NHS) probably represents the most talked-about political agenda (across a broad spectrum of public opinion) to have affected and influenced the country's last four generations. During the 1950s, 60s, 70s and 80s, the NHS was identified as one of Europe's largest employers in terms of number of employees (second only to Russia's Red Army – reported then as the largest). Today, since the fall of the Berlin Wall in 1989, it *is* now recognised as *the largest*.

There is somewhat of a dichotomy, however, as we could be led to believe that, the greater the number of employees, the more visible and expeditious the service provision to patients. The reality, though, seems to point to an NHS that is continually in need of public funding with an ever-increasing need, year on year, for greater levels of financial investment required to meet the electorate's expectations of a healthcare service delivered at the point of demand.

Gartner Dataquest (March 2003):
Market Segment Trends: Western Europe, 2001–2006 Total European IT spending will reach $495.6 billion across all market segments in 2006, representing a 4.2% compound annual growth rate (CAGR) from 2001 to 2006, despite a tough year in 2003. Healthcare and education are the areas showing the fastest spending growth. Germany and the United Kingdom spend the most on IT. The United Kingdom is the largest market for external IT services where healthcare investment as a single market segment represents a 10.8% CAGR from 2001 to 2006.

A second dichotomy is the healthcare market split in Britain between public and private funding. Approximately 85% is state-funded, 15% private. Conversely, as a general guideline across other UK market sectors, this ratio is inversely represented as approximately 85% private, 15% state-owned. In Europe, however, French and German healthcare market division, for example, equates to an approximately 60% public, 40% private ownership, whereas, across a broad spectrum of other market sectors, this ratio equates to approximately 70% public (inclusive of nationalised industries), 30% private in France and an approximately 50%/50% ratio split in Germany.

It also appears a third dichotomy is at work, in that, during the late 1940s, Britain was seen as able to afford the massive public expenditure programme required to support the concept of an NHS at a time when, in relative terms to today, the country was in a more precarious financial position following the cost burden of World War II. Yet today, notwithstanding Britain's position as the world's fourth largest economy, where personal individual wealth is at a relatively far higher level than 50 to 60 years ago, the country appears less able to afford the NHS public investment required to continue supporting future patient care expectation levels in the 21st century.

This picture was seen to be reinforced by various media polls carried out during March 2002. Since then, other pollsters have revealed similar interpretive views. The UK Government's second-term strategy of making this the period of 'delivery' on public services, with the NHS top of the list, was viewed with great scepticism by the people who will decide at the next election whether it has been a success.

Nearly half (49%) of people still think the NHS has deteriorated since Labour came to power in 1997 despite the party's claims then that there were only '24 hours to save the NHS'. Only 12% believe there has been an improvement while most of the rest (31%) think it is the same as when Labour inherited it from the Tories.

There are also big doubts about the strategy set out last year (2002) by Gordon Brown, the Chancellor, of funding improvements in the NHS through higher taxes. His budget announcement during April 2002 included a phased increase in national insurance (NI) contributions, supporting, in part, a several-billion-pound annual investment programme projected year on year for the next ten years.

Whatever route is taken, expectations that it will lead to a better health service are low. One in five seem to think that extra investment will turn around the NHS, while 65% say no improvements are likely. The *question* this poses is why an ever-increasing amount of taxpayers' money is needed for successive investment. *Answer:* Because, to a large extent, public expectation levels dictate the deployment of the latest/innovative medical electronic equipment and use of newly prescribed drugs at an ever-increasing rate. Such examples of new hardware and drugs include: electron spectrometry analysis apparatus; X-ray, CT, MRI and real-time ultrasound scanners; patient and laboratory monitoring equipment; cardiovascular, dialysis and respiratory machines; upgraded/state-of-the art patient record management IT systems, plus expensive new cancer-curing (chemotherapy) and preventive AIDS drugs etc.

In comparison to only a few new medical breakthroughs during the 1940s (e.g. penicillin, discovered in 1928 and implemented as a life-saving drug during World War II), the introduction of new technology today is growing at an exponential rate due to new exponential microchip/firmware design capabilities and time-to-market issues. 40% of annual NHS public funding today is earmarked for medical electronic/IT equipment and pharmaceuticals/drugs investment, 60% attributed to nursing/medical staff and hospital building construction/maintenance. Over the next five to ten years, this ratio is expected to invert when as much as 60% will be assigned for medical electronic/IT equipment and pharmaceutical/drugs expenditure.

Therefore, logically speaking, taxation would need to be raised in perpetuity, in order to cover the growing exponential investment costs. This poses a further *question:* to what elevated levels of taxation can any government in the world justify an appropriate increase to fund a healthcare management service for its people? *Answer:* The priority level various countries' populaces would attribute to different healthcare service elements covering, for example: euthanasia (only legal in some areas of the world, e.g. Switzerland); eugenics (only legal in some areas of the world, e.g. the USA, France and now the UK due to a House of Lords select committee decision in 02.02 and High Court legal judgement passed 04.03); and embryonic fertilisation (potentially, widely permissible). In these examples, serious ethical questions are raised/implied in parallel with the associated financial considerations. They also relay how medicine is on a collision course with the law.

Euthanasia
Ethical Case Study 1:

During the early part of 2002, it was widely reported in the British tabloid press and news broadcasting media that an elderly lady was admitted into hospital following a succession of medical complications, necessitating her being wired up to various pieces of medical apparatus, namely a dialysis machine, a cardiovascular machine and a respiratory machine. The medical staff concerned had technically pronounced her as dead all but for the machines maintaining her vital circulatory condition. As a consequence, the medics, realising the elderly lady's terminal state, conferred as to their next course of action. The consensus was that the machines required shutting down, enabling the elderly patient to die peacefully. However, all the trained medical staff concerned were reluctant to undertake this action/responsibility, knowing what the consequences might be.

Question: Who ultimately took the decision to shut the medical machines down and should the machines have been shut down anyway?

Answer: The matter was referred to the medics' legal advisors and the law judges assigned to the case at the High Court in London. Legal judgement was pronounced to the effect that the medical life-saving machines should be switched off and that the medical staff in question were absolved of any potential manslaughter charges or legal malpractice exposure resulting from the elderly lady's inevitable death.

Conclusion: The legal profession (judges/lawyers) determined the outcome of what is essentially a medical decision.

Eugenics
Ethical Case Study 2:

The study of human cellular tissue and embryonic genetics using sophisticated chemical/physical application software programs within laboratory controlled environments has for some time created high emotion and passion on both sides of the divide. It has long been accepted that the predetermined genetic characteristics/ make-up of human embryos (e.g. genetically engineered skin/eye colour, gender and either singular or mixed racial background) are linked to the preconceived notion of a master-race creation, which could alter the balance of nature's random laws.

Public disclosure in the UK during 2003 has indicated that British parents could be permitted to select the gender of their offspring under new initiatives announced by the Human Fertilisation and Embryology Authority. The agency proclaims that medical advances now provide safe methods for parents to select their child's gender before it is even conceived.

If the UK government endorses the proposals, then it would signify a major step towards the reality of 'designer babies' in Britain. The implementation would inevitably lead to fertility clinics being allowed to offer procedures such as sperm sorting prior to embryo creation for social engineering and medical reasons.

The extension of genetic predetermination can lead to the concept of reproductive cloning and raises serious ethical issues associated with identical/replicated human cell structure generation.

The reality, though, is that thousands of human embryos are earmarked to be used today in medical research by British Government scientists. They want to build up the world's first bank of cells that could be used to treat dozens of medical conditions, from Alzheimer's disease to diabetes.

The initiative has outraged many people on religious grounds, while some experts in medical ethics are appalled that the project has continued and will continue to involve the destruction of embryos on such a large scale.

It is estimated that one in six couples suffer from infertility. Couples who have subsequently undergone fertility treatment are being asked to donate embryos left over after in-vitro fertilisation (IVF). Critics claim they are being emotionally blackmailed into consenting by being told that medical breakthroughs will otherwise be delayed.

The Medical Research Council (MRC), which is in charge of the Government's scientific research funding, announced the highly contentious project on September 11, 2002. There was grave concern that the MRC had chosen such a sensitive anniversary as the launch date, with some seeing it as a cynical attempt to 'bury' the news.

Scientists claim that work on the embryonic stem cells – the body's mother cells that are capable of developing into any kind of tissue – will bring about a revolution in conventional medicine. They hope the project will allow them to lead the world in using embryos as a source of spare-part cells and organs. For example, brain cells could be produced to treat Parkinson's disease or cardiac tissue could be used to repair failing hearts.

Q: **Stem cells: What are stem cells?**
A: Stem cells are the body's 'mother' cells and have the potential to develop into any kind of tissue. In adults, they are found in the bone marrow and nervous system, but by far the richest source is the human embryo.

Q: **What can stem cells be used for?**
A: Scientists worldwide are working to find ways to change stem cells into useful

spare-part tissues. New brain cells could be produced to treat patients with dementia, new pancreatic cells to cure diabetes, or cardiac cells to repair damaged hearts. In future, it might be possible to grow entire new organs for transplantation.

Q: What is their potential?
A: Experts claim stem cells could offer such a range of treatments they could revolutionise medicine. Stem cells derived either from a patient's own bone marrow or from an embryo cloned from their cells would be perfectly matched, eliminating the problem of rejection.

An embryo is created by the fusion of a sperm and egg. With IVF, this is done in the laboratory using temperature-controlled monitoring equipment (incorporating microchip/firmware technology). British law allows scientists to experiment on embryos up to 14 days old. However, the Catholic Church believes life begins at conception and sees embryo research – even when it involves a ball of cells a few days old – as immoral. The Vatican's official newspaper describes the cloning of embryos for medical research as a 'violation that stains the blood of innocence'. It was recently acknowledged at the Catholic Bishops' Conference that, whilst advances which are going to improve the quality of life for those who suffer disease or illness were welcomed, the Catholic Church maintains that human life is sacred and the destruction of an embryo should not be used as the mechanism by which new treatments are established.

Outspoken critics of embryo research have stated that the project raised 'grave concerns' about the 'commercialisation' of the human embryo. Many believe the embryo is entitled to utmost respect and should not be turned into a commodity that is bartered, bought and held in a bank for the purposes of exploitation. There is no doubt that *technology* is being developed that will enable the harvesting of human embryos for treatments which, if they work, will be worth substantial sums of money.

Expressed views from the ProLife Alliance have indicated abhorrence towards the exploitation and loss of early human life which will be generated by this initiative. It appears as though a commercial bank in every sense of the word will be set up, and in no time we can expect market trading in human embryo derivatives, as many thousands of embryos are sacrificed.

Biotechnology firms who are advising the MRC on the cell bank are known to be encouraged about this new, groundbreaking initiative. It is now considered that there is a legislative and political framework that offers a good position compared to the US and other parts of Europe. It is also acknowledged that the MRC is working very closely with IVF clinics to ensure a steady supply of embryos for research.

As well as using embryos from IVF clinics, scientists are also creating them specifically for the purpose by fertilising eggs in the laboratory. Other scientists are now attempting to produce more using cloning. Stem cells taken from adults, which persist in the bone marrow and the nervous system, are also being stored.

In a speech to the Royal Society during early 2002, Tony Blair vowed to make Britain the world leader in embryo research.

In February 2002, a House of Lords select committee gave scientists the go-ahead to conduct more research on embryos and to create cloned embryos as a source of stem cells for transplantation. The decision, which followed several earlier votes in Parliament, made Britain's policy among the most liberal in the world.

Society should be under no illusion as to the implications of this scientific breakthrough. In South Korea, the cloning of human beings has already begun in earnest with the announcement in the journal *Science* during February 2004 confirming that genetic material from a donor had been fused in a woman's egg where the woman's intrinsic DNA nucleus had been previously removed.

The egg was artificially stimulated via electrical excitation to activate cell division. Once divided, an initial 2-cell embryo was created. The cells then continued to divide, making a 4-cell embryo. Three days later, the embryo had developed into 8 cells. Following 5 to 7 days, stem cells were removed to grow into body parts and tissue.

In this particular case, the complete process is referred to as 'therapeutic cloning' (the intent/aim to manufacture body parts and tissue). However, because the technology is present today, there is a clear and present danger that human 'reproductive cloning' may now become a reality somewhere in the world.

Medical ethicists argue that the notion of creating human life for experimentation is ethically unwarranted, others see it as a means that justifies the end as far as 'therapeutic cloning' is concerned. There are, though, those who would advocate full human 'reproductive cloning'. The pressure for this stance is anticipated to come from the IVF lobby/activists who see it as a 'right' that precedes other considerations to have children regardless of the technological method used to reproduce them. If that includes creating human replicas of themselves then so be it.

We live in a society which allows a woman to give birth to her own niece or grand-daughter and a man to father children long after his own death. Who is to say that, eventually, society won't be as accepting of human cloning – regardless of the psychological and social traumas of children born in the shadow of their genetic and hereditary past?

Question: What material benefit and added advantage would there be for either an individual or society as a whole to produce an exact replica/copy of oneself?

Answer: Some people have responded by stating that should replacement skin or limb/organ tissue be required, following, for example, a personal accident, then human cell duplication processes could provide the required remedy to the adverse condition. In addition, if the cloning technology exists, permitting an exact replication of a human being, then labour-intensive tasks assigned to the original person could be divided accordingly.

Conclusion: Human cell replication appears to offer a medical solution to an otherwise adverse intractable problem. On the other hand, the future division of labour concept seems to conjure up the idea of created humanoid armies being given their marching orders, quite literally, into battle. The problem here seems to be: what happens if the clones instruct the originals as to who does what, where and when?

In-vitro fertilisation (IVF)
Ethical Case Study 3(a):

Today, there are nine different ways in which a woman can conceive a baby without the need for a natural biological male partner, from surrogacy through to laboratory-created test-tube babies and in-vitro fertilisation (IVF) techniques.

As we have observed with eugenics, an embryo is created by the fusion of a sperm and egg. With IVF, this is done in the laboratory using temperature-controlled monitoring equipment (incorporating microchip/firmware technology).

A 1998 Government report that contains the most up-to-date information currently available showed that between 1991 and 1998 a total of 763,500 test-tube embryos were created.

Q: What currently happens to surplus IVF embryos?

A: Storage of frozen embryos is allowed for five years, but may be extended for a further five years if both partners agree. In special cases, storage is sometimes allowed for even longer if a woman is still of child-bearing age. Between 1991 and 1998, 194,000 embryos were put in storage, 238,000 were not used and destroyed, and 48,000 were given for use in research.

Q: What does the law say about it?

A: Under the UK 1990 Human Fertilisation and Embryology Act, scientists could use human embryos up to 14 days old for licensed research into fertility, contraception, miscarriages, congenital diseases and chromosome abnormalities. But the law did not permit the use of embryos for research into diseases. In December 2000, MPs voted to relax the rules, opening the door to the use of embryonic stem cells as a source of spare body tissue for transplantations and to cloning embryos in the laboratory for medical research. In February 2002, a House of Lords select committee gave scientists the final go-ahead, thereby making Britain's policy the world's most liberal.

Women who find they are expecting twins or triplets after receiving treatment for infertility are electing to have one or more babies aborted. Official Government figures reveal that 49 babies were destroyed in the womb by lethal injection in one year, usually to spare their mothers the additional burden of raising them.

The operations were mostly carried out three to four months into the pregnancies. Although some of the babies might have had defects, many would have been healthy and were chosen at random. Infertility treatments that lead to multiple pregnancies were supposed to have been restricted following the outcry in 1996 over the case of Mandy Allwood, who became pregnant with eight babies.

The disclosure that dozens of babies are being selectively killed has prompted demands for a crackdown. Eminent physicians/ fertility specialists have expressed that putting back too many embryos and then forcing patients to even consider selection reduction is ethically, medically and emotionally wrong.

According to the latest official Government figures, 40 women selectively aborted 49 babies in Britain in 2001 – and 90% of the multiple pregnancies were created by fertility treatments.

Only a few physicians are prepared to perform the procedure. Unless an individual foetus shows obvious signs of abnormality, one or more babies is selected according to how easily the lethal injection can be administered. They are terminated by injecting potassium chloride to the heart and are left to atrophy in the womb while the other baby or remaining twins develop normally.

Infertility clinics performing IVF procedures are legally permitted to implant up to three embryos. In practice, most clinics put back only one or two to avoid the risk of the mother being advised to destroy one or more unborn babies with the risk of long-term psychological damage. However, some women produce multiple pregnancies after treatment with fertility drugs prescribed by family doctors (ref. Pharmaceutical market segment use of IT application software for chemical analysis).

Some of the terminations are deemed necessary to safeguard the lives of the remaining siblings. Since 1978, more than one million children worldwide have been born through IVF. Of these, about 6,300 children are born through IVF each year in the UK. Significantly, an increasing percentage are now being born without the eventual realisation of ever knowing a natural biological father.

Question: Who is looking out for the unborn child here? What right does any one single potential mother have to decide on behalf of the unborn child that he/she (the child) will not know/have a natural biological father? (If equal rights are eventually granted by society/government, this may include, in the near future, the right for a single parent father to decide on whether the unborn child should be born without knowing/having a natural biological mother.)

Answer: Eventually, society may decide that the psychological, social and financial costs to society as a whole are too great and, therefore, restoration of a more stabilised family unit environment is what is required to hold together a more cohesive structured society.

IVF
Ethical Case Study 3(b):

During November 2003, a 39-year-old single woman from Illinois, USA, who was not involved in a biological relationship with a male partner, managed to scrape together enough money to undergo IVF treatment at a registered state hospital. She was cautioned that a 37% probability existed that the treatment may result in a multiple pregnancy due to the administered fertility drug process involved. Nevertheless, the procedure was initiated and the woman in question gave birth to quadruplets.

The resulting cost to the taxpayer included the coverage of incurred medical care expenses equating to $5,000 for each day the quadruplets remained in hospital together with many other subsequent financial state benefits (social security, housing, income support, continuing healthcare management etc.). The real tragedy, though, seems to be that not one of the four children conceived shall ever know who their natural biological father was or is. Furthermore, as a consequence, additional expenses may also be incurred by the taxpayer due to future psychological and social assistance/care given for each of the four children once the realisation of never ever knowing who your biological father was/is begins to take effect in adult life.

The rationale supporting the 39-year-old woman's decision to proceed with IVF treatment rested upon the argument that, because she had so far been unable to find 'Mr. Right' and thereby enter into, sustain and secure a relationship with a male partner, was society really saying that she should not, therefore, be allowed to undergo a process of child conception, in this case using IVF?

Question: Is not the foundation of family law in the Western world based on the concept that decisions taken should always be on the premise of 'what is in the child's best interest'? In the absence of any father's rights existing, this is a straight decision on whose rights predominate – that of the potential mother or those of the unborn child and eventual conceived child/grown adult (regardless of gender)?

Answer: 'Mr. Right' may be a long time coming, but that doesn't necessarily mean that rights should be relegated with respect to the unborn. If 'Mr. Right' never was or never has been, then conceiving children and bringing them into the world through whatever alternative means may simply be wrong and not right.

Conclusion: It is one thing for two parents (mother and father) to consciously and willingly conceive a child, and maybe, unfortunately at a later stage, for the parental relationship to break down. It is another matter when a single parent decides for him/herself, from the outset, that the rights of the unborn child are secondary (or non-existent) to the single parent's own need to fulfil his/her self-gratification, by predetermining that no additional opposite gender parent is required/necessary.

IVF
Ethical Case Study 3(c):

According to government records, of the 43,700 couples who seek IVF treatment in England alone every year, only a few manage to do so on the NHS. However, the National Institute for Clinical Excellence (Nice) in the UK have proposed free IVF for all women between 23 and 39, providing they have been unable to conceive during a two-year period. Exactly who will be permitted to access the free treatment has yet to be fully determined by the UK government, although the Nice framework specifies that any infertile woman who fits the assessment criteria would be eligible, regardless of whether she was married, single or gay.

It is important to realise that there are key decisions that have to be made; no healthcare system in the world supports the concept of everything funded for everybody.

Question: What is not going to be financed for if we pay for IVF? Should we not initially be considering paying for life-threatening disease treatments before we widen out payment considerations to include lifestyle options? Example:

According to 2003 UK Department of Health figures:

IVF Funding Costs:
6 treatment cycles required where each cycle = approx. £2k–£4k

(Minimum cost = £12k)
No. of women elected for treatment = 26,000/yr.
Total = £312m/yr.

Coronary Heart Bypass:
(Minimum cost = £9k/operation
No. of patients requiring treatment = 28,000/yr.
Total = £252m/yr.

Question: Is it not more important and a greater priority for society as a whole to care initially for the well-being of the living as far as facilitating the extension of human life, before financial investment consideration is given to the unborn? Should we not be servicing those who are currently alive before purposely creating additional human life which may otherwise compound an existing financial problem?

IVF
Ethical Case Study 3(d):

Disclosure by the broadcasting media in July 2003, announcing the consultative research between Israeli/Dutch experts at the Meir Hospital in Kfar Saba, near Tel Aviv, Israel, and Utrecht University in the Netherlands, has revealed the retention by scientists of ovarian tissue from aborted foetuses in order to test whether such tissue samples can be kept alive under laboratory-controlled conditions using microchip-based instruments that regulate temperature, atmospheric pressure and humidity levels. The end purpose is to determine if mature human eggs can be produced for IVF.

The process is currently declared illegal in the UK and many other countries throughout the world, but there is no escaping for anybody from the ethical questions raised.

Evidence that Israeli and Dutch scientists are working closely together illustrates how science and technology are now globalised.

Question: Is surely not the first and paramount need now for the emotional well-being and stability of the conceived child resulting from the eventual and inevitable knowledge/effect of finding out that your mother was an aborted foetus that had never lived?

Answer: The new scientific/technological advances demonstrate again the lead impact on social, medical (psychological) and legal issues harboured for tomorrow's successive human generations.

IVF
Ethical Case Study 3(e):

In the United States, the most widely viewed cable news broadcast, Fox News, reported in March 2003 a disturbing legal case in Michigan State. A lesbian patient (the plaintiff) was suing a female medical practitioner (defendant) for not undertaking to provide in-vitro fertilisation treatment at the request of the plaintiff, as the medical practitioner in question was refusing to conduct an IVF artificial insemination procedure on religious grounds.

The defendant had offered to refer the request for in-vitro fertilisation to another medical practitioner in the same state and was prepared to pay all out-of-pocket expenses for any inconvenience caused. The plaintiff, however, was not prepared to accept this resolution, as the plaintiff argued she had been a long-standing patient at the defendant's clinic for a number of years. In addition, the plaintiff believed her own rights superseded those of the defendant's, as the defendant held a medical practitioner's state licence, and therefore had both a moral and legal responsibility and duty to honour/uphold Michigan state's sexual/gender discriminatory laws, in compliance with the defendant's professional standing as a practising state medical doctor.

Question: Given the expected degree of tolerance that the plaintiff expects society as a whole to exercise/demonstrate towards those of different lifestyles, should the plaintiff not be expected to exercise the same degree of tolerance towards the medical practitioner in this case, given the deep-seated personal religious convictions as expressed by the defendant?

Answer: No. The plaintiff's charge was upheld and a further judicial review is now pending based upon the defendant's anticipated right to exercise the US Constitution's First Amendment.

Conclusion: It seems again that computer technological innovation/implementation has given rise to a controversial situation necessitating a legal resolution. The plaintiff may be right (yet to be determined) as far as the letter of the law is concerned, but this case is essentially the pursuit by an individual on what she (the plaintiff) wants/expects/demands, regardless of the expressed feelings and due consideration of both the defendant and society as a whole.

IVF
Ethical Case Study 3(f):

In the UK during 2002, a case was widely reported in the tabloid press and broadcasting media, involving two heterosexual women who took their claim to the High Court in London seeking legal cover to have their stored frozen eggs fertilised with their ex-husbands' sperm. Each of the women in question was divorced and both their ex-husbands were fighting the case in order to prevent their former wives from proceeding with the fertilisation as, under UK law, both partners are required to provide authorisation enabling embryo creation.

The women's claim is that they wished to finish what they had started, inasmuch as their broken marriages should not act as an impasse to concluding what they had initially instigated as an agreement with their former husbands.

The implication for both men, should fertilisation proceed, would be far-reaching, as both men, under child paternity laws in the UK, are expected to financially contribute to the eventual child's upbringing, even though their marriages had broken down and a divorce was certified under UK law prior to embryonic creation.

> *Question:* Should the women pursuing this case be allowed, in part, to seek legal aid enabling them to bring their respective claims to the High Court? And should the unborn children have a predetermined

decision made on their behalf that, whilst both a natural biological mother and father exist, the child is being brought into a living environment, in the full knowledge, from the outset, that both divorced parents are clearly unwilling to mutually cooperate together in raising the child?

Answer: Future generations will conclude the end result of future legislation and implications for society as a whole. Again, the conceived child may very well require social and psychological help later on in life, financially underwritten by future governments of the day.

Conclusion: Probably, the same result applies here as is related to Ethical Cases 3(c) and 3(e). The 'I' and 'me' factors seem to predominate at the expense of others/society in general and the impact/fallout relays how medicine continues to collide with the law.

BIOTECHNOLOGY/PHARMACEUTICAL
(Module 2)

The biotechnology and pharmaceutical market segment represents the second largest market segment in the USA today with generated sales revenues in excess of $150 billion during 2002. This is likely to increase significantly over the coming years as a result of an ever-increasing number of new therapy drugs resulting from a milestone in genetic science, the completion of the human genome.

On 14 April, 2003, six world leaders, including Tony Blair and George W. Bush, announced that the 3 billion letters of the genetic blueprint of humanity had been deciphered and mapped. This task was greatly facilitated using sophisticated chemical/spectrometry and chemical mapping/decoding computer application software.

It marks the culmination of 15 years of research that has turned human genetics from a mainly academic discipline into a science with the power to transform society and perhaps even humanity itself.

Many thousands of lives could now, for example, eventually be extended by a revolutionary new cancer treatment being pioneered in the UK. Research studies indicate that a transfusion of genetically modified (GM) engineered blood cells could give intestinal cancer patients a powerful boost against their disease. In laboratory computer-controlled conditions, the technique proved completely effective and, as a result, scientists now envisage conducting the first patient trials in the UK during 2004 with a realistic expectancy of producing a proliferated therapy soon after 2010. The remedy involves isolating a profiled type of 'T cell' which can be used to target alien body cells in general. An artificial gene is then added to the T cells to enable them to attack specific intestinal cancer cells.

Intestinal cancer:
Intestinal cancer is the second most common cause of cancer death in the UK. According to UK Government Department of Health statistics, there are 34,000 recorded cases a year – an increase of approximately 12% compared with a decade ago (1994). The disease kills more than 15,500 annually with the disease being

most common in people over the age of 50. Medics believe that the consumption of too many high sugar and fat content foods and not enough intake of fibre inclusive of fruit and vegetables is partially contributory to the rise in cases.
N.B. According to collated 2003 UK retail food statistics the average UK household spends more on alcohol per week than on the purchase of fruit and vegetables.

Human Genome
Ethical Case Study 1:

Predictive DNA health tests are part of the human genome revolution and within a decade will probably become as common as a standard blood pressure check. In principle, they offer huge benefits, alerting people to the fact that they have a propensity to specific diseases long before any symptoms emerge. By making changes to their lifestyle, diet or medication, people should be able to reduce the risk of the predicted conditions ever developing.

The procedure involves cell collection with a swab or from saliva which can provide the DNA for gene testing. The sample is placed in a sterile flask for posting back to the laboratory. Scientists then analyse the DNA to extract an individual's unique molecular signature using advanced computer mapping software. The gene tests can show you are prone to get: Alzheimer's disease, hypertension, cardiac disease, breast cancer and intestinal cancers. On the other hand, gene tests can show you *will* definitely get: Huntington's disease, muscular dystrophy, cystic fibrosis and haemophilia.

DNA:
British chemist Francis Crick and South African chemist Sydney Bremner claim to have determined the genetic structure of deoxyribonucleic acid (DNA) in 1961.

The predetermination of cellular/embryonic genetic characteristics could leave a generation of people without private medical insurance cover. Genetic science has paved the way for predictive medical analysis of an individual's life development as they advance towards adulthood. These future medical predictions could dissuade and prevent private medical insurance companies from providing medical cover and therefore, by default, impose an additional burden upon the UK's already overstretched National Health Service (NHS).

Various companies that carry out such DNA health tests claim our genes play an important role in our health and that, by electing to look at them, we are creating for ourselves the opportunity to do something about them.

Such issues are leading to increasing concern. Inevitably, a serious ethical dilemma is created: on the one side is the interest in knowing what is in your genes; on the other is the fact that such information often affects others in society and that it can also be potentially misused.

As a result, the Human Genetics Commission, a government advisory body, is pushing for formal regulations. They suggest it should be made an offence to conduct paternity tests on children without proper consent or to carry out surreptitious tests on employees to assess their disease risk.

As of April 2003, the Department of Health has been planning to publish a White Paper on genetics and health which is expected to lead to legislation in the near future. Companies at the forefront of the new gene technologies are likely to welcome regulation. They have long recognised the possible problems of unregulated genetic testing, and the risk of a public backlash.

A number of companies that helped to pioneer the sequencing of the human genome are so confident of the market for tests for Alzheimer's and cardiac failure that they are investing in the establishment of additional infrastructure designs to support their work in the UK.

Apparently, such tests are only worth undertaking because new therapies are being developed to treat or prevent such diseases. But as the tests improve so a regulatory framework is going to become increasingly more important in order to protect people's privacy and other rights.

Question: But whose rights predominate?

Answer: What many geneticists are only just beginning to realise is that the section of society their work will impact upon most is those with the least power – children.

Conclusion: As genetic testing becomes more common, it could become standard procedure to test babies, even embryos, for defects or even for traits such as intelligence and athleticism. Is this another preemptive move towards developing a mechanism that can create the concept of a master race? (ref. Healthcare Management – subsection: Eugenics. Module 1).

Contraceptive Drugs Research
Ethical Case Study 2(a): Female Gender Analysis

During the past 60 years, in particular, since the introduction of penicillin, a variety of new drugs has progressively appeared on international markets, mostly as a result of utilising computer application software which assists in the decoding of complex chemical atomic structures/formulae. All of these new drugs have resulted/evolved from initial investment programmes where achieving the maximum profit return of investment (ROI) in the minimal amount of time (covering costs of testing processes and procedures) has been a crucial factor when introducing any new drug for consumer market consumption.

The ever-increasing use of more detailed application software has generated a prolific number of new drugs in an attempt to cure a range of complaints/medical conditions from the common cold to premature pregnancy and to alleviating the affects of the AIDS virus.

In the example of new contraceptive drugs, women will be able to avoid most of their periods with a new contraceptive pill. The drug, expected to become available in the UK during 2004, enables women to have a period only once every three months. It will allow them to escape the often depressing and painful symptoms of menstruation.

The new pill uses the same compounds found in Britain's leading oral contraceptive, which has been on the market for 25 years, and is used by 60% of women on the Pill. The present version should be used for 21 days before a seven-day break.

The new contraceptive, however, is taken for 84 days at a time, alleviating women from the inconvenience of periods. The drug is undergoing final checks before its expected licensing in the USA in 2003.

New female Pill:
According to various industry market research surveys, more than 60% of women would prefer fewer periods or none at all. Sufferers from premenstrual syndrome (PMS) are also expected to benefit from the introduction of this new Pill.

Women have traditionally relied on their periods to indicate they are not pregnant. But increasingly reliable home pregnancy tests mean menstruation is no longer necessary to perform this role. The existing contraceptive pill has always been able to arrest periods if taken for longer than 21 days.

Ethical Case Study 2(b): Male Gender Analysis

A birth control pill for men is expected to be widely available by 2007.

A collaborative venture between two pharmaceutical companies has already commenced to create a contraceptive which will revolutionise family planning. Scientists have devised the new pill to halt sperm production and combined it with slow-release testosterone to ensure that men do not suffer side-effects such as mood swings and a loss of sex drive.

Male Pill:

A male Pill is much more difficult to develop than a female one because the average man generates about 1,000 sperm a minute while a woman usually releases only one egg per monthly ovulation cycle. Halting sperm production relies on a dose of the synthetic hormone progesterone. It can either be administered in an implant, which lasts up to a year, or in a daily Pill of the same hormone. Men then need a dose of testosterone because the progesterone can affect their sex drive, moods and weight.

It offers the biggest breakthrough in family planning since oral contraceptives were developed 50 years ago. The first clinical trials started in the UK during 2003 when a number of volunteers began to test it.

Scientists from the German drug firm Schering and Dutch rival Akzo Nobel, which manufactures female contraceptives, announced in November 2002 that they are pooling resources in terms of capital expenditure relating to computer technology/innovation, manpower services and knowledge/information. This will significantly improve ROI ratios.

Question: Will scientists wonder what 20 years' of continued use in society of this new male Pill may reveal? Will there be side-effects currently not anticipated, as was the case when, historically, scientists could analyse past effects the female Pill had on women? Or will our quest to facilitate sex drive us to brush aside any consideration of associated health risks or medical conditions?

Answer: Over the next 20 years, scientists may perfect even further (using computer-aided designs) techniques for reducing the creation of side-effects resulting from new discoveries of new chemical compounds/ formulae. But will this not only further exacerbate an increasing number of teenage pregnancies through cavalier/complacent contraception use, in the belief that all is well on the night?!

Ethical Case Study 3: AIDS Combative Drug Analysis

Not a poor and destitute country, but alongside South Africa Botswana is the richest country in the African continent due primarily to its natural mineral deposits – the most bountiful supply being diamonds.

The working population experiences full employment with a backdrop of a generated supporting vibrant economy. And yet today, 60% of Botswana's total population is diagnosed as HIV-positive, with a recognised certainty that by 2010 the country's population will become extinct. The World Health Organisation (WHO) has declared the region a human disaster in the making, not just for Botswana itself but for the world in general. This life-threatening situation comes in the wake of Botswana's indigenous population's refusal so far to effectively endorse/embrace its own government's given HIV education information and medical healthcare programmes.

In response to these dire circumstances, the USA, along with other Western countries, is offering to provide recently developed AIDS combative drugs before completion of final trial tests in an attempt to stem what appears to be an imminent regional/global catastrophe.

With the recognition that some of the new drugs may produce adverse unknown reactions and side effects, the plan is to implement a speedy drug administering programme in an attempt to thereby prolong human life in Botswana.

Question: Are the taxpayers of the Western economies really providing a mandate to their respective governments, supporting the use of levied taxation in a bid to stem the tide of Botswana's population's refusal/failure to adhere to/implement their own government's given HIV education information and medical healthcare programmes? In light of the indigenous population's largely ignored welfare programmes does the rest of the world truly believe that other Western governments' initiatives can make a difference? If reluctance continues on the part of Botswana's native population to adhere to the sound advice of its own government and the WHO, should a compulsory AIDS combative drug inoculation program be enforced?

Question: With any new market drug introduction, strict testing procedures/processes are deployed. Is there any boundary that cannot be crossed or any means that doesn't justify the ends? Is the use of animals, for instance, in medical drugs testing *(vivisection)* simply not acceptable under any circumstances? And should this continue to include chemical testing on animals for new cosmetic product introduction?

Answer: I fear that society's insatiable desire for new cosmetics will perpetuate the use of animals for this type of chemical/biological testing. However, there is a strong argument for continuing to use some animals in controlled laboratory regulated conditions in order to test new life-saving drugs – e.g. carcinoma and AIDS drugs.

Conclusion: Some people believe there are too many humans living on planet Earth and that the use of animals for scientific research is simply unacceptable. Therefore, if the end result is that more human beings die, then so be it. Others take a more pragmatic approach and believe that human life should be spared and prolonged as far as possible. The argument is that society places a higher value on human life than animal life.

SECURITY/INTELLIGENCE SERVICES
(Module 3)

In spite of the noted *insecurity* and fallibility of computer technology, governments/military and security intelligence agencies endeavour to deploy wherever and whenever possible sophisticated advanced computer tracking software in a variety of forms. This robust and comprehensive form of IT provides the security services with a distinct edge in their fight against terrorism and national/ international crime syndication in all its disguises.

Ethical Case Study 1:

11 September, 2001 (9/11), will remain etched upon the minds of generations to come.

One factor, though, that may escape the memory of some will be the capture of the so-called 20th highjacker in Pakistan during November 2002. His demise was brought about following a mobile phone call he made to a fellow accomplice, which was picked up via satellite intercept and transmitted on to US listening posts in Turkey, the CIA in Langley, West Virginia, and to the Pentagon in Washington.

The clue that revealed the 20th highjacker's identity was his unique voice-print signature which had been previously recorded/monitored and then later demodulated and mapped again to his original unique voice print on that fateful day in 2002.

Voice-print signature:
This is a digital electronically stored recording of an individual's speech pattern based on a unique frequency pitch and range resulting from a unique inflection and modulation of the human voice. The security/intelligence services deploy advance data compression and encryption software techniques to sample thousands of phone calls simultaneously. Security agencies then map the frequency pitch/range and use of key words/phrases akin to each language spoken in each phone call, and thereby filter out and home in, as deemed necessary, on specific individual conversations

currently using known landline and listed mobile phone numbers. A variety of security communications techniques (fixed and mobile) are used to monitor and geographically locate the source of individual telephone calls. Such methods include: *(i) Laser Bugging* – detection of minute vibrations in glass caused by verbal speech patterns; *(ii) Computer Detection* of images on computers which can be reconstructed using a 'Tempest' antenna pointed into a room; it detects radiation patterns emitted by a screen; *(iii) Submersive Water Detection Hacking* – new 21st-century submarine technology can eavesdrop on international laid phone cables submerged deep below the ocean surface, positioned on the seabed. Today, it is also possible to locate a mobile phone user's exact location anywhere in the world without the need for a conversation to be in progress. Simply by leaving the mobile phone switched on will ensure exact positioning coordinate obtainment. The tracking software technology is raising 'Big Brother' concerns among civil liberties groups, who believe it will harbour a culture of spying, enabling parents to keep a watchful eye on their children, employers to monitor their errant employees and married spouses to determine each of the other's whereabouts. Controversially, the tracking companies offering the service secure their information from the largest mobile phone networks (Vodafone, Orange, MMO_2 and T-Mobile), who provide the data for a set price.

N.B. Alternative profiling comes by way of individual digital fingerprinting and unique individual digital iris/retina scan analysis.

Unified messaging:
The real-time cross-transference of voice data to either written e-mail, fax or text messaging data formats and vice versa.

Ethical Case Study 2:

Internet crime has risen year on year since the Internet's early inception during the 1990s. In particular, since we have entered the 21st century, public awareness of fraudulent and pornographic crime is now at an all-time high. There is a growing school of thought that something must be done, and fast, to protect the innocent – the unsupervised or unparented child.

The FBI in America, during early 2003, provided to the British security services financial transaction evidence of credit card holders in the UK who have accessed known suspect global websites in their attempt to successfully download information of a denigrating and corrupting nature.

Thousands of named individuals have been listed in a crackdown to stamp out exploitative crime, which is seen as potentially harmful to today's young child population. Over time, these same children will become tomorrow's adult generations, and therefore, in order to curtail the effect of each future generation potentially multiplying its problems, preventive action now has been decided.

Preventive monitoring action:
In the absence of any firewall technology, governments around the world have the ability today to monitor hit list websites and user root paths connecting those individuals who access suspect Internet addresses. The sophisticated viewing software permits governments/security intelligence services to monitor which Internet software functions each user is using.

Question: Do innocent people stand the risk of erroneous accusation given the incessant and perpetual struggle to combat terrorism wherever it manifests itself worldwide? Could technology be misused for the wrong purposes if it were to fall into the wrong hands?

Answer: Providing individuals' telephone conversations remain innocuous, then we should fear not. However, those who are guilty of violating human laws should refrain from believing that safety is found in numbers. The pinpoint technical accuracy with which an individual can be located today, via either website or mobile phone intercepts, may mean that you can run but you cannot hide.

Trusting the security services to prosecute in a fair and balanced way is paramount to the stability of democratic government/society. Where the security agencies are accountable for their actions under law and to various government private select committees/ chambers, society has to believe that any security service rogue activity will be dealt with in accordance with the established principles/ guidelines laid down by democratic government/ elected representatives. However, in autocratic government, the situation may be vastly different where unelected representatives are not ultimately accountable to the people.

Ethical Case Study 3:

The use of DNA (genetic fingerprinting) (ref. Biotechnology/ Pharmaceutical Module 2) is proving increasingly important in the fight against crime. It is used to confirm the personal identification of individuals required by the security services. Example: Having located and captured Saddam Hussein in Tikrit, Iraq, in December 2003, DNA testing was used to verify with certainty Saddam's identity, given the number of lookalikes that could otherwise have claimed Saddam Hussein's same physical characteristics.

A number of police cases/enquiries have been solved using this very potent tool in conclusively convicting the guilty individual/ parties concerned. This is achieved by collecting hair and skin cell tissue, and articles of clothing with DNA cell deposits on material fibre (inclusive of carpets, wood-flooring etc.), at the scene of the crime.

As reported in the tabloid press and by the broadcasting media at the time, a classic example follows British military intelligence and SAS collusion in pinpointing the whereabouts of alias 'Chemical Ali' in the Iraqi War (Gulf War II). This reprehensible individual was responsible for gassing the Kurds during the 1980s and brutally repressing the Shi'ite uprising immediately after the First Gulf War in 1991. Following the deployment of a precision-guided bomb on Chemical Ali's palace in Basra, Southern Iraq, during April 2003 (Operation Iraqi Freedom), it was necessary to establish conclusively his resulting death. This was undertaken by retrieving part of Chemical Ali's torso and conducting a DNA test. The results, though, later proved negative/non-affirmative.

Ethical Case Study 4: Unified Database Technology

During the Christmas and New Year period 2003, intelligence security reports indicated that Islamic terrorists intended to hijack a passenger plane to use as a missile. As a result, foreign visitors arriving in the United States were for the first time electronically fingerprinted and photographed. The security procedures are now expected to become standard and routine at all US international airports. The details will be kept on a computer database, available to dozens of US law enforcement and intelligence agencies. The introduction of the 'biometric' checks has fuelled instant criticism from various civil liberties groups, who see this particular security measure as another example of civil rights infringement.

Even before departure of an international-bound flight to the US, the airline carrier from the departing city is now required to e-mail the list of all passengers embarked on a US-bound flight to anti-terrorist authorities for checking purposes. Unfortunately, delays have been imposed on the travelling public due to incompatible computer software adaptations existing between the FBI and other different security agencies' networks required to complete passenger ID authentication. Inevitably, this is expected to lead towards the establishment of a unified centralised database to which all government agencies can eventually gain intelligence access.

Question: Are my civil liberties compromised if DNA information is obtained/collected by the security services without my knowledge or approval?

Answer: Providing the hair/skin/material fibre etc. is obtained/collected at the alleged crime scene and you are a suspect, then that is one thing. It is another matter if the security services require taking a sample of your DNA directly from you for matching purposes, as the security agencies would require your permission. This may, therefore, cause a problem in determining whether you were present at the crime scene and, given this circumstance, the security agencies may seek to obtain the necessary and appropriate legal cover in order to complete their work.

Conclusion: There is much speculation as to whether Britain will move towards a centralised computer database, holding all DNA profile information of each and every citizen in the UK. If this was to materialise, the security services would argue that such centralised DNA information would greatly facilitate their fight against crime. Again, could this potentially powerful store of digital information be misused and the wrong individual genetically fingerprinted for adverse/corrupting/political reasons? The same implications apply here as with arguments detailed in Ethical Case Studies 1 and 2. Currently, the United States is deliberating the same implications. Should, say, the Federal Government elect to allow the FBI, INS and Homeland Security access to centralised stored DNA information pertaining to its citizens? Ethical Case Study 4 illustrates the technological freeway to centralisation we have embarked on, where electronically stored fingerprints and photographs can lead to digitally stored genetic DNA records.

TRANSPORTATION
(Module 4)

Microchip implantation incorporating the latest firmware designs provides numerous opportunities to both register and record information in real time, whether for medical application use (via cardiovascular pacemaker technology, ear-drum membrane replacement and visual optical aids) or for criminal and child tagging procedures which allow for the monitoring of individuals within a given perimeter range.

Microchip tagging:
Silicon microchips are biophysically inserted below the skin surface tissue.

In another example, the UK Government, in March 2003, announced it had placed an order for three new armour-plated Jaguar custom-built cars to protect the Prime Minister and his entourage from ambush by al-Qa'ida terrorists using poison gas or high explosives. Air cylinders provide electronically regulated and temperature-controlled oxygen flow inside the car.

The James Bond-style Jaguars feature the latest ultra-security microchip-driven gadgets. Although each car will weigh more than three tons, they have specially adapted suspension systems so they can travel at 150mph.

The core of the car, designed around the passenger compartment, can withstand the blast of a Nato-standard hand grenade and bullets from high-velocity automatic rifles. Devices fitted to the wheels will allow it to continue moving at speed even if the tyres have been shot out.

The car's security system will detect whether anybody has tried to interfere with or enter the vehicle. An intercom with speakers under the car allows those inside to communicate to people outside without having to open the windows.

As the world moves into an increasingly uncertain 21st century, automobile microchip implementations will become more standard, particularly in areas of security applications.

Ethical Case Study 1: Traffic Congestion

In Tokyo today, the Japanese Government has decreed that Japanese automobile manufacturers insert coded microchips within motor car registration number plates. The reason is to allow monitoring of vehicles passing through specified entry and exit points along the city mapped grid system.

Using Global Positioning Satellite (GPS) tracking software, each car is registered at the point of entry and exit, thereby determining journey time duration and the map routing of each vehicle at a given time of day or night.

Transportation information is then used where possible to improve the flow of traffic and thereby reduce vehicle congestion.

Vehicle congestion:
London's Mayor, over time, may elect to implement a similar GPS electronic grid system, comparable to that in Tokyo. In addition to monitoring and regulating traffic flow, the implemented tagging system could provide a more efficient means of securing congestion charge collection, car insurance, road tax, MOT, car ownership and address updates.

Ethical Case Study 2: The Informant Microchip

Without a camera flashing, and with no policeman to flag you down, a concealed chip in your new car was registered by radio wave technology, collating information on your every move. This is not some futuristic vision but a plan, as reported in the broadcasting media during 2003, set out in official UK government papers that could begin to pave the way for implementation by 2007.

The UK government is pioneering broader consideration of this new microchip/barcode/mini-satellite transmitter technology known as Electronic Vehicle Identification (EVI) ahead of other regions in the world, including Japan, in terms of its alleged benefits and merits to government and society as a whole. Discussions have currently centred on the possible introduction in the UK of tolls on roads after 2010 and on the fact that motorists could be tracked and charged by Global Positioning Satellite (GPS). Inevitably, additional monitoring information could be obtained, which clearly makes road revenue generation only a small part of a far wider agenda.

The police and security services argue that EVI will allow them to track suspect terrorists, drug criminals or car thieves together with identifying those motorists who have not paid their car insurance or road tax or whose MOT certificate has expired. Whatever the case or justified interest in reducing crime and at the same time increasing safety, EVI is set to evoke an emotional debate about how far civil liberties should be infringed.

The UK government has already conducted discussions with various third-party mobile phone, computer, car and boat manufacturers in determining ways to best facilitate the implantation of microchips in registration plates, including the implementation of microchip cameras inside a vehicle body chassis. This particular form of EVI will allow date, time and location stamping of motorists' individual journeys, coupled with image and voice identification/registration of passengers in every vehicle.

Question: Is this not an encroachment upon personal individual freedom? If a government can monitor an individual's whereabouts in terms of where and when he/she travelled and for how long each journey time was spent transferring from one location to another, is this not sensitive information that the individual alone should know about, and not something to be shared with Big Brother?

Answer: Yes, in a word. But . . . there could be an argument under extenuating circumstances that would override consideration of personal civil liberties if acts of terrorism or violent crime are committed. Then, government authorities may elect to evoke restraining powers that could assist the security services to track and apprehend a suspect criminal/terrorist (ref. Security/Intelligence Services – Module 3).

Conclusion: Continual endeavours must always be made to strike a balance in deploying technology just for the sake of convenience as opposed to use for protection of a nation's security.

Ethical Case Study 3:

A number of scientific leaps throughout the course of aviation history have conclusively demonstrated how computer software-driven technology has impacted on the aviation industry. One such evident use was the introduction of flight simulation recorders. This amazing technological innovation allows airline and fighter pilots to train in simulated real-life modes: practising take-off and landing procedures, coping with and confronting different in-flight manoeuvres, recovery from unexpected catastrophic engine failure and restoring aircraft control lost due to either mechanical or electrical performance failure, or resulting from adverse weather conditions.

Almost all the potential life-risking events and circumstances associated with air travel can now be controlled and dealt with through extensive instruction sessions which aim to lay down the ground and flight rules prior to pilots engaging in real-life situations. Even qualified pilots are still required to consistently train on flight simulators by continuing to book time with qualified flight instructors to gain further flying hours' experience.

It is, therefore, surprising to note a trainee flight instruction case recorded in the United States during 1999/2000 involving a major American airline and a female trainee pilot who, at the time, was completing her final flight simulator examination.

All trainee pilots, regardless of gender, are given three attempts to pass out on the flight examination. If failure to pass on the third attempt is encountered, there is no graduation ceremony.

In this particular case, the female trainee pilot had unfortunately flunked the first two attempts and was now re-scheduled to take her third, last attempt. Halfway through the last attempt, she informed her instructor she felt under pressure and expressed how she was being subjected to an adverse level of stress/strain in order to pass. At this point, her flight instructor started to shut down the simulator and informed her she would have to find herself another flight instructor.

As a result, the airline concerned allowed the trainee pilot to re-take the third/final attempt of the simulator examination under the supervision of a new flight instructor. She did so, but later failed the final re-taken third attempt.

The airline company, in an attempt to propitiate and to be seen as empathetic and conciliatory, decided to grant the trainee pilot a fourth opportunity to successfully complete the failed third attempt of the examination. Once again she failed.

She then proceeded to sue the airline company on grounds of sexual harassment and discrimination based upon differentiation between herself and her male colleagues who were only given three attempts to pass the simulator examination as opposed to her four.

The reality was: even if the airline company had retained its 'three strikes and you're out' policy, the trainee pilot, in all probability, would still have litigated. Either way, it appeared a no-win situation for the airline.

The financial sums were done and all totalled, after securing sworn affidavits, written testimony and issuing of subpoenas inclusive of management time involved etc., the cost would have exceeded $750,000. Due to financial constraints, the airline company therefore settled out of court, and paid $100,000.

Question: What is more important here? The safety rights of the fee-paying airline passenger public or the alleged employment rights of a trainee pilot?

Answer: The air passenger public's safety rights are paramount and should always override all other considerations. The trainee pilot was clearly not of a high enough calibre to have been entrusted with responsibility for airline passengers' lives.

Conclusion: Fortunately, flight simulator recorders allow employer/employee issues such as these to be addressed and resolved on the ground rather than in the air! But this does raise important concerns relating to employer/employee working relationships/business politics and associated employment law which have been primarily affected and generated as a result of computer IT innovation.

MILITARY WEAPONS ESTABLISHMENT
(Module 5)

According to the United Nations (UN), during the past 58 years, between the end of the Second World War until the present time (2003), more wars have been fought and prosecuted during this intervening period than in any other relative period throughout the entire course of human history. More than 250 individual wars and insurgencies have been conducted, resulting in the deaths of more than 8.6 million people.

Sample war listings include:

Arab/Israeli War – 1948	(Est. dead: unconfirmed)
Korean War – 1950/51	(Est. dead: unconfirmed)
Suez – 1956	(Est. dead: unconfirmed)
Cuban Missile Crisis (Bay of Pigs) – 1961/62	(Est. dead: unconfirmed)
Vietnam War – 1964/72	(Est. dead: 500,000?)
6-Day War (Arab/Israeli) – 1967	(Est. dead: unconfirmed)
India/Pakistan/Bangladesh – 1971	(Est. dead: unconfirmed)
Uganda – 1972/76	(Est. dead: unconfirmed)
Yom Kippur War (Arab/Israeli) – 1973	(Est. dead: unconfirmed)
Cambodia – 1972/74	(Est. dead: 1.5 million?)
Angola – 1974/75	(Est. dead: unconfirmed)
Afghanistan/USSR – 1981	(Est. dead: unconfirmed)
Iran/Iraq War – 1981/88	(Est. dead: 2.0 million?)
Falklands War – 1982	(Est. dead: unconfirmed)
Ethiopia – 1985	(Est. dead: unconfirmed)
Lebanon – 1986/87	(Est. dead: unconfirmed)
First Gulf War (Kuwait/Iraq/UN) – 1991	(Est. dead: 200,000?)
Rwanda – 1994	(Est. dead: 1 million?)
Somalia – 1994/95	(Est. dead: unconfirmed)
Balkans War (Kosovo/Serbia/USA/UK) – 1995	(Est. dead: unconfirmed)
Sierra Leone – 1997/98	(Est. dead: unconfirmed)
Afghanistan/USA/UK – 2001/02	(Est. dead: 150,000?)
Second Gulf War (Iraq/USA/UK/Aus/Pol) – 2003	(Est. dead: 100,000?)

These are staggering statistics by any proportion and yet paradoxically confusing to understand.

We may pride ourselves on the fact that since World War II successive generations of people are better educated and, dare we say, more sophisticated than previous generations; and yet we seem to have developed, within and for ourselves, an ability to inflict more harm on humanity than previous generations could ever have imagined.

We have devised more technically efficient and effective means by which to wage war and bring destruction and destitution to the innocent, whose only dream is to live as one and in peace.

It seems, in many respects, that the speed of technological innovation has outpaced the psychological and social development of the human race, and many are left wondering – what are we to do?

I am reminded of the 1960s American singer/songwriter Bob Dylan, whose lyrics of one song seem to transcend the years/decades and encapsulate the sentiment of time:

> *. . . How many years can some people exist,*
> *before they're allowed to be free?*
> *Yes, and how many times can a man turn his head*
> *and pretend that he just doesn't see? . . .*

> *. . . And how many ears must one man have,*
> *before he can hear people cry?*
> *Yes, and how many deaths will it take 'til he knows*
> *that too many people have died?*

> *The answer my friend is blowing in the wind,*
> *The answer is blowing in the wind.*

(Bob Dylan – 1962)
(Words and Music by Bob Dylan, published by kind permission of Special Rider Music/Sony/ATV Music Publishing)

The struggle for power underlies almost every conflict of our day from the clash of great nations to industrial disputes. For power is a dangerous thing, which in our lifetime alone has devastated the world, torn nations apart and in the process destroyed the personalities of those who have used it wrongly.

In the final analysis, there are only two forms of power in the world: power over people (compulsion) and power with people (persuasion). And civilisation could be described as man's attempt to replace power over people by power with people – compulsion by persuasion, regimentation by education. In contrast, much of man's history throughout the 20th century and before was seen to be dominated by compulsion and regimentation, leaving an embittered legacy of conflict affecting hundreds of millions of people.

The Roman Empire provides a classical example of the clash of these two forms of power as was seen in the Judgement Hall when Pontius Pilate confronted Jesus Christ. Pilate had the power to command men's bodies – the power of death. Christ symbolised the power to win men's hearts and minds – the power of life. And Pilate was to discover that what he had always believed was the ultimate form of power was simply ineffective. He could break a thousand men's bodies but could not break one man's spirit.

Earlier civilisations and empires, from the time of ancient Babylon (originally established as the Biblical Garden of Eden – now modern Iraq), have risen and fallen only to leave a common thread of continuity stringing any possible sense or meaning together – namely, the human condition – the lust for power and control.

Garden of Eden:
Ref. The Bible: Genesis Ch.1

Nebuchadnezzar was an ancient Babylonian king whose kingdom was found 'wanting and divided' – predictions of his plight were foretold by ancient 'hand-writings on the wall', illustrating the division of Babylon into the Media and Persian empires. Geographically transcribed into modern Iraq, following the fall of the Turkish Ottoman Empire in World War I, Saddam Hussein met a similar demise when prediction of his eventual military defeat was outlined by today's only world superpower, the United States. His country already divided by the enforced no-fly zone 32nd parallel in 1991 (effectively providing autonomy to the Kurds), Saddam's major tank divisions of the Republican Guard (aptly named amongst others in a historical context – the Medina and Nebuchadnezzar Divisions) were no match for America's weapons in 2003.

Nebuchadnezzar:
Ref. The Bible: Daniel Ch.5

Saddam Hussein:
'Saddam' in Arabic means 'one who confronts'.

Ironically, the newest weaponry created by man was deployed in/on the oldest civilisation known to man. Laser or satellite-precision guided bombs with an accuracy to within ten feet, cruise missiles and cheap unmanned drones that can decimate any defence, Apache helicopters used as tank-busters or the 'massive ordinance air blast' (Moab) bombs – the largest non-nuclear bomb yet produced – all served to prove the point in military superiority.

'Smart' ordinances:
E-Bomb: High-powered microwave warhead (HPM) on cruise missiles releases up to 2 billion watts, destroying any electronics within 1,000ft. Microwaves penetrate bunkers and scramble computers.
Blackout Bomb: Showers power stations with carbon graphite filaments, short-circuiting and disabling grids. First bomb used in 1999 against Serbia, where only 20% of the country's power was restored after 24 hours.
JDAM: Joint direct attack munitions smart bomb is a converted dumb bomb with minicomputer and fins which allow GPS systems to steer it within 10ft. of target. More than 90% of bombs were smart compared with 10% in the First Gulf war.
Moab (the Giant Daisy-Cutter): The massive ordinance air blast is the world's largest conventional bomb. It is launched from the rear of a C-130 transport plane and contains 21,000lb. of explosive. Blast devastates everything within a 1-mile radius.

Paveway Penetration (Thermobaric) Bomb: Laser-guided bomb specifically designed to destroy hardened bunkers; 4,400lb. warhead, 19ft. long. Designed to drive through 100ft. of ground or 20ft. of concrete. Delayed fuse explodes bomb after deep strike. Releases intense heat at low pressure inside bunker – prevents dispersal of deadly chemical and biological agents.

Mobile Laptops: Provide commanders with a 3-D view of urban streets and potential sniper positions. Air strikes called in to neutralise perceived dangers.

Military Satellites: Synthetic aperture radar satellites have infrared cameras and can see through night or bad weather. Can identify a single vehicle. They also monitor enemy mobile and satellite communications.

Storm Shadow: The European cruise missile as used for the first time in Iraq by the RAF. The Boeing C-17 can be used to launch missiles using parachutes, or direct from an internal bomb bay.

As the centuries have rolled on, lessons have been wasted on us. We still try to use power over people to do what can only be achieved by power with people. But as recent technological warfare advances have developed, so has a different emphasis in its execution and result been detected – winning the loyalty of men and women without violating their freedom.

Operation Iraqi Freedom (Second Gulf War – 2003) has revolutionised the mode of warfare. The American battle plan was to deliver 'shock and awe'. Its wider war plan was to bring humanitarian aid, reform and justice to the Iraqi people. Its wider strategic interests demanded that it deliver a quick, clean, legitimising victory to a sceptical world outside.

For these reasons, this war emphasised psychological operations, media imaging and discriminate destruction. The blitzkrieg that followed used an ordinance of cutting-edge technology incorporating the latest solid-state microprocessor and software designs. The resulting battle progress led one BBC commentator to enquire on 5 April, 2003, at Central Command Headquarters in Doha, Qatar: 'Will this be the first war in history to end before the cause of the war is found?' (namely, weapons of mass destruction – WMD).

The First Gulf War of 1991 was the last significantly sizeable war of 20th-century military forces. In 2003, the Iraqis were still locked in that preceding era but the United States was now fighting a different, 21st-century campaign.

General Tommy Franks, the American commander, echoed the assertion at the time, by Donald Rumsfeld, the US Defence Secretary, that this is 'network-centric warfare' where 'commanders at all levels have a total picture of the theatre of battle and can deliver troops, equipment and destruction anywhere, anytime, in any weather.'

In 1991, 10% of the weapons used by the allies were smart guided weapons. In 2003, the proportion was at least 90%. Above all, the military revolution lies in the software that integrates command and control. American crews work from laptop computers inside their tanks, accessing the tactical picture in a sector, and since the late 1990s the US has been integrating its newest battle-field command software into its infantry divisions.

The fundamental change in military strategy is largely concerned with what can be destroyed, but the impact in political terms that has accompanied it over the past decade is more concerned with what should not be destroyed. This balance between destruction and reconstruction is now continually evaluated for maximum effect.

Operation Iraqi Freedom was an immense test of new technology, serving more complex political and military doctrines, in a geographic region where issues of global power and descent were genuinely at stake. It proved to work and Iraq was freed.

The *question* now is: can the peace be won, and not just in Iraq?

Question: Does any government have the moral right or justification to wage war on another, or is warfare of any description simply unacceptable in today's world?

Answer: Pacifists will argue the case for non-violence regardless of the cause or provocation. Others will argue the case for self-defence, and some, pre-emptive action to ultimately prevent the need for self-defence.

Conclusion: There is a time for war, there is a time for peace. There is a time to be silent, and a time to speak. There is a time for all things. And in the general scheme of things, regardless of the cause, the high moral ground cannot always be justified simply on the basis of inaction; no blood spilt, no conscience to clear. Sometimes, an equally devastating cause and effect is inaction itself. In some cases, equally as important as what *is* said and done is what is *not* said or *not* done. Therefore, each dilemma confronted has to be wrestled and reckoned with on this account.

THE MUSIC AND ENTERTAINMENT INDUSTRY
(Module 6)

As recently as the early 1980s, it was inconceivable to think how digital sound and visual reproduction technology could ever have led to the extensive impact on recording techniques as is demonstrable today.

Without discernible loss in sound or visual quality, coupled with the physical compactness compact disc (CD) technology provides, digital recording and playback facilities have revolutionised an industry which prior to the last twenty years seemed immovable from the analogue age.

Mobile digital recording studios have taken on a new dimension in that, two decades ago, the only real way to cut a record was to buy studio time, which was prohibitively expensive due to the limited number of professional recording studios available to artists. Those artists who believed they had written suitable material worthy of recording either had to raise sufficient finances themselves or hope to get spotted and have the recording company underwrite the expense.

The opportunities now affiliated with low-cost audio digital equipment provide the means by which artists can achieve the same high-quality digital recording in the home environment as can be obtained/produced in a professional sound studio, managed by a major record label.

With audio/visual material now creatable in a digital format, the transmission of sound/optical content across the Internet provides instantaneous accessibility to new material. Music can be downloaded via MP3 file format and burnt on either CD-R (Recordable) or CD-RW (Read-Write) and then either played back on a CD-drive or transferred to a variety of other digital reproduction systems.

This does, however, raise controversial issues associated with artists' intellectual property rights (IPR) (ref. The Context – subsection: The Historical Context – Root Module). The record companies today plan to release CDs with in-built technology that prevents people from making copies for friends or putting albums onto the Internet for anyone to pirate. New albums will carry warnings that they contain devices which may stop them being played on computers.

They are part of a concerted campaign by the record industry, which claims that home copying is costing it up to £1 billion a year in Britain alone.

Some record companies have experimented with promotional CDs that have included devices to turn off the copying functions on computers. Since November 2002, many of the CDs released commercially in the UK carry copy-controlled technology with clearly displayed warnings or a new anti-piracy logo.

At least four different technologies are being used (e.g. Cactus Data Shield), varying from preventing play on a PC to limiting distribution of music on the Internet.

During 2001, 308 million blank recordable CDs were sold in Britain. The industry estimates that of these about 128 million discs were used to copy music rather than computer programs. Sales of commercial CDs aggregated 220 million in the same year.

The biggest selling album in the USA during 2001 was Linkin Park's Hybrid Theory with 4.8 million CDs sold. But a single Internet site offering the album free had 4.3 million hits.

In the long term, massive copying deprives musicians, authors and composers of their very livelihood. New trends and talents can only emerge if music is bought legitimately and the proceeds from sales are then invested in the development of new music.

As the record industry continues to battle against Internet music and video pirating, the Recorded Industry Association of America (RIAA) has asserted that the era of major artists' pop albums selling in high volumes is now at an end. Coupled with increased market pressure from supermarket chains selling CDs at discount rates and attracting more and more consumers away from buying at traditional record stores, the big five record companies (Sony Music, Universal Records, Bertelsmann (BMG), EMI and AOL Time Warner) recognise they have a real sales revenue problem. The issue is further compounded by the fact that music as a commodity product has to compete with other consumer goods such as TVs, DVDs, computer games and mobile phones etc. on a dollar/pound for dollar/pound basis.

In a wider bid for market share, Cable & Wireless is introducing during 2004 a music-download service in collaboration with Britain's largest retailer Tesco, selling pop music over the Internet. In America, Apple's market-breaking iTunes service, which has reportedly sold 30 million songs in seven months since its initial inception, and Coca-Cola's similar launch of its own Mycokemusic.com service in collaboration with OD2, has clearly prompted the decision for C&W to endeavour to emulate this same degree of success in the UK.

Unauthorised file-sharing services:
The record industry estimates that when combined downloading software plus peer-to-peer services (computer users swapping music with each other) are taken into account approximately 2.5 billion files are copied each month.

For the struggling or not-so-famous artist, rather than representing a means of lost income, the Internet could in fact act as a persuasive promotional medium. Whilst sales in traditional established music tastes have declined, rap and hip-hop have, in comparison, increased in generated units sold. Consider for instance the following:

Ethical Case Study 1:

Ludacris may well be a household name to some, but for the uninitiated a word of explanation is probably required.

A well-established rap musician with roots in New York, Ludacris started recording music several years ago. His recognition was enhanced via Internet transmissions of his songs and the ability of many supporting fans to download MP3 formated digital files of his music material.

Proliferation of rap amongst other forms of music on the Internet is rampant, to the point where any age group can access, record and duplicate at will. The problem seems to be quite literally that unparented, unsupervised young children (11, 12, 13 years) are subjected to the lyrical content of some songs that are highly questionable.

Fox News (America's most widely viewed cable news broadcast) recently highlighted (late 2002/early 2003) the problems associated with some lyrical music forms, where, in particular, Ludacris was cited following the hiring of his services as a promotional agent by Pepsi-Cola.

Fox News (O'Reilly Factor) claimed it was wrong for Pepsi-Cola to sign-up Ludacris to promote their products because it sent the wrong message to young kids. In Fox News channel's opinion, Pepsi-Cola's action appeared to condone the use of Ludacris' lyrics expressing the incitement to violent behaviour by men towards other men/women and use of abusive language. As a consequence, Fox News advocated to the viewing public that the competitive soft drinks product Coca-Cola should be purchased by the consumer. Within a week, it was announced by Pepsi-Cola that Ludacris had been dropped as their promotional agent. I wonder why? The power of the greenback and media/public persuasion, perhaps?

Ironically, the advertising medium that Pepsi-Cola hoped to exploit to increase sales revenue was the very medium used against them to achieve a different result.

Question: Who looks out for the unparented, unsupervised child who has a free rein of the Internet and who can listen to or view whatever material he/she selects? Is it Ludacris? Is it the record companies? Is it Pepsi-Cola? Is it those manning the websites?

Answer: No, no, no and no to the above. They all appear to act with impunity.

Conclusion: Regardless of whether rap music is considered a legitimised art form or a sub-culture movement that warrants recognition, 20 years ago the record companies did not produce lyrically turgid material, simply because it would not have been granted airtime for play. Today, however, the record companies' position is compromised, as any loss of income due to non-airtime play by the broadcasting media is supplemented by the free promotional effects of the Internet.

The big issue here still remains: who does really care for the interests of the unparented, unsupervised child?

SPACE INDUSTRY
(Module 7)

Space – the final frontier.

In 1961, the 35th President of the United States (John Fitzgerald Kennedy – JFK) declared that, by the end of the decade, America would land a man on the Moon. 'We chose to do this', he said, 'not because it is easy but because it is hard to do.'

What ensued was an unprecedented period of technological advance, heralding, for example, the development of the world's first 8-bit minicomputers using early assembler language compiler designs. These initial 8-bit computer innovations, built around small-scale integration (SSI) and later medium-scale integration (MSI) semi-conductor technology, contributed largely to the Apollo space mission guidance and tracking system's success. Without this mathematical invention, man's voyage to the Moon would have been filled with danger, if not just simply impossible to achieve.

The motivation to put man on track to the Moon by the end of the 1960s was, in part, politically and technically inspired by a competitive race. Both Russia and the United States invested trillions of dollars and roubles, each trying to outmanoeuvre and outsmart the other to achieve this objective.

However, the true beginnings of the Space Race can be traced back further to World War II when, in October 1942, a brilliant young German scientist by the name of von Braun, together with many hundreds of Germany's best physicists and mathematicians, developed the world's first vertical take-off rocket using liquid hydrogen and oxygen fuels. The vertical rocket superseded the earlier designed horizontal propelled rocket; they were named the V2 and V1 rockets respectively (Hitler's 'revenge' weapons). Although the guidance systems were primitive by today's standards, they still achieved their aim with chilling results as experienced by London's population during 1944/45. Travelling faster than the speed of sound, the V2 payload explosion preceded the sound of its arrival.

V1 rocket:
Conceptually, this was the forerunner to the modern cruise missile, which tracks the Earth's geographical contours using guided global positioning satellite (GPS) microprocessor navigation technology.

Following the Allied victory and fall of Germany in April 1945, von Braun and 150 of his fellow scientist colleagues surrendered to the Americans outside Peenemünde in Germany. They were later transported by American forces to Alabama in the US where America proceeded to embark upon its rocket programme under a shroud of secrecy (Operation Paperclip).

The Russians, however, were the first to launch a satellite into space in 1957 (Sputnik), later followed by the first living creature (a dog – Laika) during the same year and the first human astronaut in 1961 (Yuri Gagarin). In 1962, however, America launched Telstar, enabling live television pictures transmitted from Andover, Maine, to be received at Goonhilly Down, Cornwall, SW England, and in Brittany, France.

This initial lead the Russians appeared to develop really cajoled the United States into taking the quest for space exploration very seriously. Hence JFK's announcement referenced in 1961.

It inspired a brief poem, which captured the sentiment and expressed feeling at the time:

> *I'm sure you've heard or read about the satellites in space,*
> *How Russia and the United States are in a rocket race.*
> *To hear them talk it won't be long till space they'll conquer soon,*
> *But just what next will man attempt if man should reach the Moon?*
> *(author unknown)*

This led some philosophers and theologians to assert that it's not the Moon or Mars we need to reach but God, who put them there!

This did not stop the venture though. Notwithstanding the universal backdrop at the time, where the 1960s represented one of the most politically and socially turbulent decades in history.

When the 'Eagle' flight capsule did finally land on the Moon on

20 July, 1969, Neil Armstrong's famously recorded remark, 'One small step for man, one giant leap for mankind', took on tremendous significance. We can now look back and see spin-offs which space travel has spawned, from space biology and medicine to the designs of dust-free manufacturing processes/techniques associated with semiconductor innovation, or the codification of laws to govern our journeys to other planets as well as the nature of our claim to extra-terrestrial territory. Certainly, these achievements have created much of what we call progress. But when a significant proportion of the world's wealth was and still is spent on man's quest into outer space, whilst vast tracts of the Earth remain desolate in poverty and squalor and two thirds of its population remain underfed, then maybe serious questions and priorities need to be reassessed.

Population parameters:
Examples:
(i) Ethiopia – 80% of the population is registered as living under the world's poverty line; 1 in 5 children will die through malnutrition before they reach the age of 5 years. The average adult age of death is 37 years.
(ii) 60% of the world's wealth is owned by 6% of the world's population – and they all live in the United States.

Question: Has a bitterly divided world the moral right to export its dissensions to another planet?

Question: Must we look forward to the Moon's Sea of Tranquillity being divided between those nations on Earth whose own divisions down here are not yet resolved for export up there?

Question: Does it not seem that nothing is ever going to change for those people living in a world of grief down here whatever the perception of a world there might be out there?

Question: Can we not use more technical skills to care for our own life-form down here on Earth rather than redirect resources in hoping to find another life-kind out there?

Answer: It seems, throughout the entirety of history, that the cause for man has got to be bigger than man himself. Regardless of what is or has been – his reach must exceed his grasp (JFK speech, 1961). This is why we ascend the highest mountains and descend to the depths of the deepest oceans. This is why man's venture into space and urge to conquer the unknown is an acknowledgement of what separates man from the rest of the animal world. His ability to dream a dream and his uniqueness to think an idea is a monument in itself to man's separation from other life-forms as we know them down here on Earth. But what about new discoveries out there? . . .

In spite of America's deficit in 2003 of $477 billion and an estimated $2.45 trillion deficit accrued by 2014, NASA officials have vowed, following the loss of the Columbia space shuttle in February 2003, that the shuttle would fly again. Many have expressed their determination to go back into space despite the shuttle programme's indefinite suspension. They believe in human exploration and they believe in the need to return to the Moon and build a space station and the need to travel to Mars.

A space probe built in Britain – the Beagle 2 Mars lander – was launched in May 2003, at the start of its journey to Mars, where it was planned to seek signs of extra-terrestrial life.

The Beagle 2 Mars lander represents the most high-profile part of Mars Express, a £100m European Space Agency mission.

Although it has reached Mars its instruments have since malfunctioned and it will now not be possible to tell whether life ever existed there. If evidence is eventually found on a planet as arid and hostile as Mars, some researchers believe, life could exist all over the universe.

The project pushes technology to its limits. Five days before it reached Mars in December 2003, Beagle 2 was ejected from its parent craft Mars Express and hurtled into the Martian atmosphere. A heat shield was designed to protect it as it decreased speed from 12,000mph to 1,500mph before parachutes opened to slow its descent to the Martian surface.

Beagle was the smallest spacecraft so far, and had the highest density of microprocessor-based instruments, including cameras, a robot arm, a drill for taking rock samples and tiny ovens to heat them to high temperatures.

Following its release and loss of Beagle 2, Mars Express will nevertheless continue to orbit the planet for nearly two years, probing the surface and atmosphere. Its computer-controlled instruments include ground-penetrating radar that will show where any Martian water is located.

Mars has apparent evidence of frozen ice caps and other water deposits. The radar will determine, as suspected, if the water has sunk into the soil and frozen. The assumption being that, if a large quantity of water is found, it would make transporting humans to Mars far more feasible.

Whatever the political and technical misgivings and whatever the financial reservations, it would still appear that man is destined for a voyage deep into space. What was considered nothing short of science fiction only thirty years ago appears today to be a definite certainty. With the completion of five further Apollo manned missions to the Moon by 1972 following Neil Armstrong's initial step onto the lunar surface three years earlier, it now seems that America is braced for another giant leap of faith with the announcement by President George W. Bush in January 2004 that the USA is committed to achieving a successful manned mission to Mars by 2030.

The announcement has already been compared to John F.

Kennedy's vision of 'landing a man on the Moon and returning him safely to the Earth' by the end of the 1960s. The difference here is that the Moon is only a three-day excursion away from Earth and not a six-month journey. The enormity of the task ahead for NASA and military strategists is immense by comparison. And yet, in spite of all, man is going because of man's insatiable desire for new knowledge and his need to seek answers to questions about the universe and the origins of mankind.

Another prompt to American success is China. The country put its first astronaut into space in 2003 and could prove to be a serious contender to any race to get to Mars. The prospect of the red flag on the red planet may further cajole America into throwing more funds at the space exploration project. Opinion shared by a number of investment banks is that China's economy will be larger than any in Europe by 2007 and will overtake Japan's in 2016. It will be second only to America during the race to Mars and is predicted to finally overtake and become the world's largest economy in 2041. The advanced military development associated with such a vibrant growing economy is clearly enough to make America, with the rest of the world, ponder the consequences of such a possible achievement.

Estimated costs of a manned mission to Mars equate to approximately $1 trillion over the next 25 years with the initial erection of a manned space station on the Moon below the lunar surface. The moonbase is then expected to act as a staging post for the eventual journey to Mars. The astronauts on the expedition will be away from Earth for at least 3 years.

By comparison, at a stroke, if these levels of financial investment were deployed on Earth and the same political will exercised to implement, many of the world's economic and social welfare problems could be eradicated.

Conclusion: It is ironic that our voyage into outer space demands that we look at many aspects of our earthly life with a new significance. We may have discarded long ago, for instance, biblical findings as hopelessly out of date and unscientific, but as the decades have passed, particularly during the 20th century with many substantiated archaeological discoveries using carbon-dating computer processes pertaining to the Earth and Moon (rock formation and dust particle analysis), we may start to realise a new perspective and meaning. For we may find that far from exceeding the reach of ancient thoughts we are only now beginning to catch up with them. So it could be that, within the discarded covers of an old book misplaced, there is contained the only adequate philosophy for the Space Age.

The well-known philosopher Bertrand Russell once said: 'It is necessary to care deeply about things which will not come to pass until long after we are gone.' Man's unique dignity encompasses not only a debt to the past but also a respect for the future. He is able so to be in the present that – when the final structure of things stands revealed long after he is gone – what was actually stood for will either stand or not stand the test of time.

The new vision of the future, adhered to by many pioneers and explorers, has largely determined the displayed mood of thinking at that time in history. Maybe what is needed now is a new examination of our own motivation and understanding.

The change from what is good for me now to what is beneficial for future generations to come would mark a move from *myself* to *yourself* and represent more than a mere matter of spelling. It would demonstrate a decisive shift in the centre of our universe.

FUTURE SNAPSHOT
(Module 8)

It is rapidly becoming the most controversial new science of the 21st century. It is called 'nanotechnology', a process that creates tiny molecular-size machines – 'nano-robots' – 1/80,000th of the width of a human hair or one billionth of the size of a human being.

The nano-robots could in theory create a process of self-replication, thereby providing a means of eradicating carcinogenic tumours, sustaining high health levels in perpetuity, innovating high-speed computers and developing new lightweight polycarbonates.

Nanotechnology research (2003):

The billion-dollar nanotechnology industry has already created transistors the size of a molecule.

Financially backed with government funding to the tune of $3.8 billion in the USA, Europe and Japan.

The figure is expected to rise to $930 billion by 2012.

It has been claimed as a small miracle beyond belief and imagination, and yet some are labelling it despicably evil, a threat that could lead to the extinction of the human race.

The fear centres on attempts to produce nano-robots which can identically self-reproduce by consuming the atoms around them. Sceptical opponents state a 'grey-goo' scenario could occur if millions replicate themselves unheeded, transforming atomic structures around the globe into similar nano-robots using embedded firmware processes.

Many in the computer IT industry view this with extreme consternation and apprehension, and believe that it represents an evil unparalleled – repercussions permeate well beyond that which conceived biological, chemical or nuclear weapons of mass destruction. It is a terrifying nightmare situation of which most people are still unaware.

Technologies are being designed that might well have the ability to consume and dismantle ecosystems.

The idea behind nanotechnology was conceived by quantum physicist Richard Feynman in 1959, when he predicted future computers would be so small as to interact with single atoms and carry out surgical cellular remedies invisible to the naked eye.

The mathematical theory is that if the first replicate (nano-robot) could manufacture a copy of itself within a defined time, the two replicates could then construct two more in the next same defined time period. Eventually, in days their weight would be measured in tons, in a short time following (fraction of a day) their combined mass would outweigh the Earth and in a matter of hours thereafter would exceed the weight of the entire solar system.

However, nanotechnology to date (2003) has been implemented in Pilkington's self-cleaning glass, and will soon be applied within invisible bar codes, self-repairing and non-porous materials such as those used in some clothing fabrics, LED and LCD mobile phone displays and absolvent silicon gauze for medical applications.

The other concern is whether nanotechnology raises ethical, safety and environmental issues not regulated as is already seen, for example, with environmental issues relating to toxic waste, medical codes of conduct and industrial work practice regulations.

Question: So is it just a small 'intelligent' molecule or something more sinister? Is this micro-manipulation of enormous benefit to mankind or a prediction of consequences unimaginable?

Answer: Whatever the case, it is bound to result in intense debate and opinion divided.

SUMMARY

The inevitability of technological change is a foregone conclusion.

Technology is, though, and should remain a conduit – a means to facilitate the end-purpose to the mutual benefit and advantage of society as a whole. It is, by the same token, an expression and reflection of ourselves, evidence of which has been demonstrated in this book.

When I consider my entry into the computer IT industry 25 years ago, I recall seeing a 32-ton computer, which could multiply long multiple-digit numbers in thousandths of a second. It was astounding – yet even more amazing is the 32-ounce human brain which conceived the idea in the first place! And even more incredible is how the same 32-ounce human brain, over time, perceived how to translate the processing power of a 32-ton computer onto an area no larger than the physical size of my fingernail!

Ultra-large-scale integration (ULSI):
Today, approximately 4 million transistors can be chemically/physically etched onto a single silicon chip (one single transistor is almost molecular in size).

Each stage of technical development requires human interaction. At this phase in microprocessor development, you can still only obtain from a computer what you design and effectively feed into it, although, as was indicated in the Future Snapshot (Module 8), this may change on the evolutionary scale over the next 20 years. Therefore, at present, and as history has already graphically shown, the effects of technology will depend largely upon man's input and ultimately what he elects to do with the end result.

The impact of deployed technology across various market segments has led me to outline, in part, examples which I believe best depict the human dilemma and the stark choices incumbent on us all today. Some are controversial by nature owing to their personalised effect on our lives. Others are extremely alarming, given the potential impact on the young in society.

Invariably, you the reader/listener will determine the best course of action, if any, that should be taken as each generation passes on its unsolved questions to the next.

In the final analysis, technology will follow where we will *IT* to lead.